Barbecue

COOKBOOK

R&R PUBLICATIONS MARKETING PTY LTD

Acknowledgements

Major Credits

Published by:

R&R Publications Marketing Pty. Ltd

ACN 083 612 579

PO Box 254, Carlton North, Victoria 3054 Australia

Australia wide toll free 1800 063 296

E-mail: info@randrpublications.com.au

Web: www.randrpublications.com.au

©Richard Carroll

Publisher: Richard Carroll

Project Manager: Anthony Carroll

Food Photography: Garry Smith

Food Stylist: Janet Lodge

Assistant: Grace Castauro

Recipe Development: Ellen Argyriou

Creative Director: Chiara Goya

Design: Richard McKellar

Proof Reader: Fiona Brodribb

The National Library of Australia

Cataloguing-in-Publication Data.

Argyriou, Ellen

Barbecue Cookery

Includes index.

ISBN 1 740 222067

EAN 9 781740 222068

1. Barbecue Cookery. 1. Title

641.578

This edition printed October 2003

Computer Typeset: Titles-Bauer Bodoni; Ingredient Humanist 521 Bold/Light

521 Extra Bold; Page Numbers Aldine 721 Text Shelly Allegro.

R&R Publications Marketing, Carlton North, Victoria, Australia

Printed in Singapore Saik Wah Press Pte Ltd

The Publishers would like to acknowledge and thank MasterFoods of Australia for their support and assistance with the provision of materials for photography and the produce for photography and recipe development.

The Publishers acknowledge the registered trademarks of Effem Foods Pty. Ltd. used in this book: MasterFoods; MasterFoods Squeeze-On, Prima, Kan Tong, Dolmio and Uncle Ben,s.

All recipes were developed on barbecues provided by:

Weber-Stephen Products Co., Breville Electrical Appliances and Sunbeam Electrical Appliances.

Contents

3

Introduction

Barbecue cooking is part of the modern way of life. Long before the new barbecues were introduced, people were slapping on steaks and sausages on many a makeshift barbie in the backyard and the forests. Two rows of bricks and an iron grill placed across the top was the usual self fashioned backyard barbie.

The backyard barbies are still with us, upgraded to appliances of various degrees of performance and sophistication, and elevated in status from the 'backyard' to the pool area, terrace, patio, balcony and even a special garden barbecue area.

All types of barbecues will produce delicious foods, and barbecue cooking is a relaxing way of cooking which is also fun. Family and friends gather around to socialise and cook at the same time. . The purpose of this book is to help you get the best from your barbecue experience.

The book is divided into sections according to cooking times. The 'Quick Cook' section will give you many ideas for barbie parties, foods which can be produced quickly for a crowd with maximum flavour. The 'Medium Cook and 'Long Cook' will help you produce outdoor family meals and entertaining a few friends. The 'Gourmet Barbecue Grill' brings the barbecue into the kitchen to make use of also used outdoors, electric barbecue grills with a hood or lid and the smaller electric table grills.

So light up the barbie, throw on the steaks, slap on the marinade and enjoy.

Ellen Argyriou

4

Tools of the trade

Handy Barbecue Tools

Don't forget that barbecues get hot, so it is important to have the necessary tools and equipment ready before you begin. Set up a table near the barbecue to lay out the necessary items.

Items of Most Importance for Safety

- Long tongs to move glowing coals or to reach across the hotplate or hot grill to turn foods.
- Long handled flat lifter to lift and turn hamburgers, egg and fish.
- A turning spatula, side and strong to turn hamburgers and flatten them as they cook.
- Insulated gloves for adjusting hot rracks, hot vents or anything else too hot to touch.
- Long handled basting brush.
- Fish grill or fish cage to make turning whole fish safer and easier.
- A bucket of water on stand by for any emergency.

Additional Helpful Items:

- Foil baking trays to cook vegetables in or use as a drip tray
- Wire cake rack to elevate foods away from heat
- Basket shaped roasting rack for meat roasts or chicken
- Adjustable roasting rack - for same purpose
- Cool handle pot for heating marinades or sauces

Cleaning the Barbecue

Never leave the barbecue uncleaned, the residue will corrode the grill and plate if left for a length of time. Check with manufacturers instructions as the materials used may differ. Most barbecue grills and plates are cleaned with a stiff wire brush and cold water. Electric barbecue grills are cleaned with a plastic scouring brush and water. Clean all barbecues while still warm, if makes the job easier.

Cooking Times

Fish and Seafood

Ensure that fish has been thawed correctly. Test grill for medium. Fillets, fish steaks and whole fish should be placed on a slightly oiled grill basket, sheet of foil or tray directly over preheated coals (direct grilling), or over a drip pan for indirect grilling.

Cook with or without hood as specified in the directions as grill type. When done, fish should just begin to flake easily when tested with a fork; scallops and prawns should appear opaque. All temperatures have been taken with a meat themometer.

Form of Fish Grilling	Weight, Size, or Thickness	Temperature	Direct Grilling Time	Indirect Grilling Time
Dressed fish	255g/9oz to 750g/1²/₃lb	70°C/160°F	9–12 minutes per 255g/9 oz	20–25 mins per 255g/9 oz
Fillets, steaks cubes (for kebabs)	1cm/¹/₂ in to 2¹/₂cm thick	70°C/160°F	4–6 mins per 1cm/¹/₂ in thickness	4–6 mins per 1cm¹/₂ in thickness
Sea scallops (for kebabs)	(6 to 7.5 per kilo/2¹/₄lb)	70°C/160°F	5–8 mins	5–7 mins
Prawns (for kebabs)	Medium (10 per kilo/2¹/₄lb)	70°C/160°F	5–8 mins	5–7 mins
	Jumbo (6 to 7.5 per kilo/2¹/₄lb)	70°C/160°F	10–12 mins	8–10 mins

Beef, Pork, Veal or Lamb

Prior to grilling it is best to trim excess fat from the meat. Test the temperature of the grill to medium heat. For direct grilling, place the meat on a grill rack directly over pre-heated coals, or if indirect grilling over a drip-pan. Grill meat uncovered (for direct) or covered (for indirect). for the time given in the scale below, or until desired doneness.

Steaks, Chops and Cutlets: Press the meat surface with tongs; if it is springy to the touch, the meat is cooked to rare, if less springy, the meat is cooked to medium, if firm with a slight spring to the touch, the meat is well done.

The temperatures given in the scale below have been taken using a meat thermometer.

Form of Meat	Thickness	Doneness Temperature	Direct Grilling Time	Indirect Grilling Time
Boneless sirloin steak	1cm/¹/₂ in	Med rare 60°C/140°F	14–18 mins	22–26 mins
		Medium 70°C/160°F	18–22 mins	26–30 mins
	2¹/₂cm/1 in		32–36 mins	32–36 mins
			36–40 mins	36–40 mins
Ground meat patties	1cm/¹/₂ in (4 per 500g/17¹/₂oz)	No pink remains, 70°C/160°F	14–18 mins	20–24 mins
Steak (blade chuck, top round)	1cm/¹/₂ in	Med rare 60°C/140°F	14–16 mins	5–7 mins
		Medium 70°C/160°F	18–20 mins	60–70 mins
	2¹/₂cm/1in		19–26 mins	50–60 mins
			27–32 mins	1–1¹/₄ hrs
Steak (rib porterhouse, rib eye, sirloin, T-bone, top loin & tenderloin	1cm/¹/₂ in	Med rare 60°C/140°F	8–12 mins	16–20 mins
		Medium 70°C/160°F	12–15 mins	20–24 mins
	2¹/₂cm/1in		14–18 mins	20–22 mins
			18–22 mins	22–26 mins
Pork chop	¹/₂ cm/¹/₄ in	Medium juices run clear, 70°C/160°F	8–11 mins	20–24 mins
	1cm/¹/₂ in		25–30 mins	35–40 mins
Lamb chop	¹/₂ cm/¹/₄ in	Med rare 60°C/140°F	10–14 mins	16–18 mins
		Medium 70°C/160°F	14–16 mins	18–20 mins
Kebabs	¹/₂cm/¹/₄ in cubes	Medium 70°C/160°F	12–14 mins	16–18 mins

Poultry

Make sure poultry has thawed correctly, rinse and pat dry with paper towels. Test for medium temperature on grill. Place poultry on grill rack, bone side up, directly over preheated coals (direct) or over a drip pan (indirect). Indirect is especially helpful with skin-on as it prevents flare-ups. Grill poultry as directed in the scale below, until it reaches the desired temperature (as meat themometer), ensure that no pinkness remains. Turn poultry over half way through the grilling time.

Type of Poultry	Weight	Temperature	Direct Grilling Time	Indirect Grilling Time
Chicken broiler-fryer or duck half	750g/1½lb	80°C/175°F	40–50 mins per 255g/9oz	1-1¼ hrs per 250g/8 oz
Chicken breast half, skinned and boned	155g/5oz each	75°C/165°F	12–15 mins	14-18 mins
Chicken or duck quarters	90g/3oz total	80°C/175°F	40–50 mins	50-60 mins
Meaty pieces	750g/1⅔lb total	80°C/175°F	35–45 mins	50-60 mins
Ground poultry	1½ cm/1in thick patties (4 per 500g/17½oz)	70°C/155°F	14–18 mins	20-24 mins

Vegetables

Before grilling, prepare and precook vegetables as directed in the scale below. To precook in a saucepan, bring a small amount of water to the boil and add vegetables, simmer, covered for the time specified in the scale.
Ensure grill is medium to high temperature. Brush vegetables with olive oil, butter or margarine and place on a lightly oiled grilling tray, piece of foil, or directly on the grill rack, directly over heat source. Grill uncovered for the amount of time specified in the scale, or until required tenderness. Watch to ensure vegetables do not char.

Vegetable	Preparation	Precooking Time	Direct Grilling Time
Asparagus	Snap off and discard tough bases of stems	2–4 minutes, then tie in bundles with string or strips of cooked green onions tops	3–5 mins
Beets	Trim; cut 1cm/½in thick		25 mins
Broccoli and Cauliflower florets			5–10 mins
Carrot, whole or baby	Diagonally slice 2½cm/1in thick	3–5 mins	15–20 mins / 3–5 mins
Corn on the cob	remove husks; scrub ears to remove silks; rinse pat dry		20–30 mins
Eggplant	Cut off top and blossom ends; slice crosswise 1cm/½in thick		8mins / 6–8mins
Fennel	Snip off feathery leaves cut off stems	10 mins, then cut into 6–8 wedges	8 mins
Leeks	Cut off green tops; trim bulb roots; remove tough outer layers	10 mins, or until tender, then halve lengthwise	5 mins
Mushrooms whole or sliced			7–10 mins
New Potatoes	Halve crosswise	10 mins, or until almost tender	10–12 mins
Onions	Slice 5mm/⅕in thick		8–10 mins on tray 3–5 mins directly on grill
Pattypan squash	Rinse; trim ends	3 minutes	20 mins
Potatoes or Kamuras (sweet potatoes)	Slice 2½cm/1in thick or 5mm/⅕in thick	10 mins, then wrap in foil	8–10 mins
Zucchini or yellow summer squash	Cut off ends; cut lengthwise into quarters or slice 5mm/⅕ in thick		5–16 mins

Types of Barbecue

Cooking Methods for Barbecues

Direct Heat Method – This is the traditional barbecue method where food is cooked directly over the heat source on the grill bars or hot plate. It sears the meat, seals in the juices and produces a characteristic chargrilled appearance. Fatty meats may cause flare-ups on charcoal and gas barbecues if cooked on the grill bars. If this occurs, move meat to the hot plate after searing on both sides or place a sheet of heavy duty foil under the meat, if a hot plate is not available. Direct heat is suitable for thinner foods which will cook quickly.

Pre-heat the grill with flame or burners on high. When flame settles down or gas heat has reached a constant temperature, adjust the burners to the temperature noted in the recipe.

Indirect Heat Method – The heat source is indirect, that is the food is placed on the grill bars with the heat coming from the sides, under the bars instead of directly under. It is a slower method of cooking than direct heat and is suitable for thicker cuts to large roasts and whole chickens. A drip tray is placed in the centre between the heat source to catch the drips. Fatty meats are best cooked over indirect heat a there are no dangerous flare-ups.

Pre-heat the grill with flame or burners on high. When flame settles down or gas heat has reached a constant temperature, turn-off the centre burners and adjust the side burners to the temperature noted in the recipe. If using a charcoal barbecue, arrange hot coals evenly on each side of the charcoal grate. Place food in the centre of the cooking grate. A drip pan is useful to collect drippingsthat can be used for gravies and sauces, it will also prevent flare-ups.

Adjusting Flat Top and Electric Barbecues for Indirect Cooking

Fuel - Charcoal and Briquette – Rake the coals to each side and place a drip tray in the centre. Cook thicker slices of meat after searing on direct heat. Roasts can not be cooked on the flat top.

Gas – Light the burners at each side, leaving the centre burner unlit. Thicker cuts may be seared over direct heat and moved to indirect heat to finish cooking.

Electric Barbecue Grills with Hood or Lid – Place a wire cake rack on the grill bars to stand 22cm/9 in above the bars. Place large cuts, roasts and whole chicken in a foil baking tray and stand on the wire rack. Cover with hood or lid and cook for the required time.

Barbecue Cooking Information

Cooking Times – Although the recipes in this book have been tested on a variety of barbecues, cooking times should be considered as a guide or approximate, because of the many variables which can effect the time. These include;

1. Thickness of meat - indication of thickness has been given in the recipes, but your choice may differ. Cook to the degree of doneness desired. See testing for doneness following.

2. Wind factor - will effect gas barbecues as flame is blown sideways thus effecting the temperature of the grill bars or hot plate.

3. Temperature of the food - room temperature and refrigerated meats will differ slightly in time.

4. Quantity of food being cooked - a full grill of hot plate of food will cook a little slower than a few pieces.

5. Type and quantity of fuel - the different barbecue fuel products have varying heat output. Check with supplier. Cook to required doneness instead of solely on time.

Types of Barbecues

Weber® Master-Touch™ Barbecue Kettle

Patented one-touch system that automatically opens and closes all vents with one simple movement. The patented Tuck-away™ lid has a meat thermometer that tells you when the meat is cooked perfectly. Comes with a full colour comprehensive owner's handbook, charcoal rails and drip trays.

Breville Ultimate Health Grill

Designed in Australia featuring "Steak Sear Control" system with 2400 watt non-stick char-grill and 12 heat variable control plus Steak Sear Setting. Great for either inside or outside grilling. Options include a Grill Stand and a Roasting Hood (as shown in photograph)

Sunbeam Kettle King

Comes with powerful 2400 watt element embedded in the hotplate, ensuring fast heat-up, even heat distribution and long element life. Non-stick cooking surface, ribbed and flat hotplates, thermostatically controlled, removable probe, removable drip tray, cooltouch handles, moulded base, high domed lid with steam vent and weatherproof parts to allow outdoor storage.

Weber® Flat-Top

The Weber® Flat-Top is really exciting. The quality of workmanship and materials is superior to any barbecue we have tested. The sliding enameled surfaces are a great idea, they come together to form a weather-proof lid. It also measures how much gas is left in the gas bottle. The patented cooking system lets you flame grill without those massive fat fires. A great innovation!

the quick
cook

Quick cooking on the barbecue to feed family and friends...easy preparation made possible with the many new sauces and marinades available today.

Foods in this chapter are all cooked over DIRECT HEAT and take 4 to 15 mins to cook on flat-top barbecues, placed on chargrill bars or on a hot-plate. All types of fuel barbecues may be used, including charcoal, heat beads, briquettes, gas and electricity. An electric barbecue grill or griddle plate, heated over an electric or gas range may be also used.

For the quick cook, thinner steaks, chops, thin sausages, skewered meats, fish and poultry are used and all take from 4 to 15 minutes to cook. Simple quick ideas for the backyard barbie.

Quick Sausage Sizzle

This method is suitable for cooking a large number of sausages to serve around. Pork or beef thick sausages are used, which are simmered in water before placing on the barbecue. This prevents the thick sausages from splitting and reduces the cooking time on the barbecue. Calculate the amount of sausages needed for the number of people to be served.

Ingredients
2kg/4½lb pork or beef sausages   honey & chilli marinade (page 89)
1kg/2¼lb onions, thinly sliced

Method

1. Place sausages in a large saucepan and cover with cold water. Heat slowly until simmering point is reached, then simmer for 5 minutes. Drain well. If not required immediately refrigerate until needed.

2. Heat the barbecue until hot and grease grill bars with oil. Pour the honey and chilli marinade into a heatproof bowl and place at the side of the barbecue. Arrange sausages from left to right on the grill bars or hotplate and brush with the marinade. Turn and brush with marinade after one minute and continue turning and basting for 10 minutes until sausages are well glazed and cook through. Give a final brushing with marinade as they are removed to a serving platter.

3. To cook onions, oil the hot plate and place on the onion slices. Toss at intervals, drizzle with a little oil as they cook. Serve the honey and glazed sausages with the onions and accompany with salad and garlic bread (page 84).

Lamb Satays

Ingredients

2kg/4lb boned shoulder of lamb
I cup satay marinade (page 89)

Dipping Sauce
$^1/_4$ cup satay marinade (page 89)

Method

1. Cut the lamb into $^1/_2$ cm/$^1/_5$ in cubes. Place into a non-metal bowl and stir in $^3/_4$ cup of marinade. Cover and marinate for half to one hour, or longer in the refrigerator. Soak the skewers in hot water for $^1/_2$ hour

2. Thread 2 or 3 lamb strips onto each skewer, using a weaving action. Spread to cover $^2/_3$ of the skewer only.

3. Heat barbecue until hot. Place an overturned wire-cake rack over grill bars to prevent marinade charring the hot grill. Arrange the skewers in rows on the wire rack and cook for approximately 8–10 minutes, turning frequently. Brush remaining marinade from the bowl over the lamb during cooking.

4. Thin down the remaining marinade with extra coconut milk, place in a heatproof bowl and heat on the barbecue. Remove skewers to a platter and drizzle immediately with the heated marinade.

Yields approximately 30 skewers

Cajun Cutlets

Suitable for all barbecues. Ideal for electric grill/barbecue.

125g/4½oz butter

3 teaspoons cajun seasoning

1 small red chilli, seeded and chopped

12 lamb cutlets

1 tablespoon olive oil

Method

1. Beat the butter to soften and mix in 1½ teaspoons of the cajun seasoning and the chopped chilli. Place butter along the centre of a piece of plastic wrap or greaseproof paper to one centimetre thickness. Fold plastic wrap over the butter then roll up. Smooth into a sausage shape and twist ends. Refrigerate to firm.

2. Trim the cutlets if necessary and snip the membrane at the side to prevent curling. Flatten slightly with the side of a meat mallet. Mix together 1½ teaspoons of the Cajun Seasoning and olive oil then rub mixture well into both sides of the cutlets. Place in a single layer onto a tray, cover and stand 20 minutes at room temperature, or longer in the refrigerator.

3. Heat the barbecue or electric barbecue grill to high. Place a sheet of baking paper on the grill bars, making a few slashes between the bars for ventilation. Place cutlets on grill and cook for 3 minutes each side for medium and 4 minutes for well-done. When cooked, transfer to a serving plate and top each cutlet with a round slice of Cajun butter. Serve immediately with vegetable accompaniments. (see vegetable section page 55)

14

Teriyaki Tenderlions

Ingredients

455g/1lb chicken tenderloins
teriyaki marinade (page 89)

Method

1. Place tenderloins in a non-metal container and stir in about $^1/_2$ cup teriyaki marinade. Cover and marinate for 30 minutes at room temperature or place in the refrigerator for several hours or overnight in the refrigerator.

2. Heat the barbecue until hot. Place a sheet of baking paper over the grill bars and make a few slits between the bars for ventilation, or place baking paper on the hot plate. Place the tenderloins on grill and cook for 2 minutes on each side until cooked through and golden. Brush with marinade as they cook. Serve immediately with extra teriyaki marinade as a dipping sauce.

Serving Suggestions:

1. Serve with steamed rice and vegetables.

2. Toss into salad greens to make a hot salad. Dress salad with 1 tablespoon teriyaki marinade, 1 tablespoon vinegar and 3 tablespoons salad oil.

3. Stuff into heated pocket breads along with shredded lettuce, cucumber and onion rings and drizzle with an extra spoonful of teriyaki marinade.

Toasted Steak Sandwiches

A great favourite for backyard barbecue gatherings or fun family meals. Flat-top barbecues the hot plate or kettle barbecues are best. May also be cooked on electric barbecue grills. For each sandwich allow 85g/3oz of raw steak per serve.

Ingredients

455g/1lb topside steak
2 tablespoons lemon juice
1 teaspoon crushed garlic
salt and pepper
1 tablespoon oil

butter for spreading
10 slices toasted bread
2 large onions, thinly sliced
1 tablespoon oil
steak sauce of choice

Method

1. Cut the topside steak into 4 or 5 pieces and pound with a meat mallet until thin. Place in a non-metal container. Mix the lemon juice, garlic, salt, pepper and oil together and pour over the steaks. Turn to coat both sides and marinate for 30 minutes at room temperature, or longer in the refrigerator.

2. Soften the butter and spread a thin coating on both sides of the bread. If desired mix a little garlic into the butter.

3. Heat barbecue until hot and oil the grill bars and hotplate. Place onions on the hotplate. Toss and drizzle with a little oil as they cook. When beginning to soften, push to one side and turn occasionally with tongs. Place toast on hotplate and cook until golden on both sides. Place steaks on grill bars and cook 2 minutes on each side.

4. Assemble sandwiches as food cooks by placing steak and onions on one slice of toast, topping with a good squirt of steak sauce and closing with second slice of toast.

Yields 5 sandwiches

Chicken Patties served on
Basil Flapjacks with Chilli Yoghurt Sauce

Ingredients

Patties
455g/1lb mince chicken
$^1/_2$ teaspoon salt
$^1/_4$ teaspoon pepper
1 teaspoon crushed garlic
$^1/_2$ teaspoon fresh chopped chilli or chilli powder
2 tablespoons dried breadcrumbs
$^1/_4$cup water

Flapjacks
1 cup self-raising flour
$^1/_4$ teaspoon salt
2 tablespoons chopped basil
1 teaspoon crushed garlic
$^3/_4$ cup milk
1 egg
Chilli Yoghurt Sauce
200g/7oz natural yoghurt
2 teaspoons sweet chilli sauce or to taste
mix well together

Method

1. Mix all patty ingredients together and knead a little with one hand to distribute ingredients and make it fine in texture. Cover and rest in refrigerator for 20 minutes. With wet hands, form into small flat patties about 2$^1/_2$cm/1in in diameter. Place on a flat tray until needed and refrigerate.

2. Prepare batter for flapjacks. Sift the flour and salt into a bowl. Mix together the Blended Basil and Garlic and the milk, then beat in the egg. Make a well in the centre of the flour and pour in the milk mixture. Stir to form a smooth batter. Cover and set aside for 20 minutes.

3. Heat barbecue until hot and oil the grill bars and hotplate. Brush the patties with a little oil and place on grill bars. Grill for 2 minutes each side,cook the flapjacks at the same time, pour $^1/_4$ cup of mixture onto the greased hotplate. Cook until bubbles appear over the surface and the bottom is golden. Flip over with an eggslice and cook until golden. Transfer to a clean towel and cover to keep hot.

4. Serve a flapjack on each plate and arrange 3 patties on top with a dollop of chilli yoghurt sauce.

5. Serve with a side salad and the extra flapjacks.

   Serves 6

Barbecue Breakfast
Sausages, Eggs, Bacon, and Basil Tomatoes

Ingredients

8 thin sausages

$^1/_4$ cup honey and lemon
marinade (page 91)

4 rashers bacon

4 small tomatoes, halved

2 tablespoon chopped basil

1 clove garlic crushed

1 teaspoon vegetable oil

4 eggs

4 slices of toasted bread, lightly
spread with butter on both sides

Method

1. Heat the barbecue grill bars and hotplate. Brush with oil or spray with oil spray.

2. Place the sausages on the grill bars and turn to lightly sear on all sides. Place a square of baking paper on part of the hotplate and move sausages onto the paper. Brush with the honey and lemon marinade as they cook. Turn frequently and cook for 8–10 minutes. Place bacon on hotplate, grill until cooked. Blend together the chopped basil, garlic and oil, spread onto the cut surface of the tomatoes and place on the hotplate.

3. Break eggs into egg rings on the hot plate. Cover with a saucepan lid to glaze the top. If the barbecue being used has a hood or lid, place it over barbecue for a few minutes while eggs are cooking. Toast bread on both sides on the grill or hotplate. Serve immediately. Serves 4

Marinated Barbecue Steaks

The cuts labelled 'Barbecued Steaks' by your butcher are those less tender and more economical cuts from beef (cross cut blade, osyter blade, topside, silverside), lamb (fore quarter), and pork (fore loin). For best results, they need to be marinated for 12 hours or more in an acid-based marinade. To ensure adequate time, it is best to place steaks in marinade overnight in the refrigerator.

Ingredients

2kg/4$^1/_2$lb barbecue steak or
chops 1$^1/_2$cm/$^1/_2$ in thick

herbed wine marinade (page 89)

Method

1. Cover the base of a non-metal flat container with some of the marinade, put in the steak, cover with marinade and, if necessary, place other slices on top and cover with more marinade. Cover with plastic wrap or lid and refrigerate overnight. Before cooking, stand at room temperature for 30 minutes.

2. Heat the barbecue to moderate and oil the grill bars. Remove steaks from marinade and drain well. Place a large sheet of baking paper on the grill bars, and make a few slits between the bars for ventilation. Place on the steaks and cook for 5 minutes, turn and brush top with marinade. Turn again after 5 minutes, brush with marinade, then turn and brush each minute for a further 5 minutes until the steaks are well glazed and cooked as desired.

Serve with barbecued vegetables or salad.

Pork Chops with Chilli Rice and Glazed Apples

Ingredients

1 cup soy & honey marinade (page 90)

6 pork loin chops 1½cm/½ in thick

salt and pepper

2 large apples, cored and cut into thick rings

2 teaspoons chilli powder

3 cups cooked rice

Method

1. Trim fat from chops as desired and sprinkle lightly with salt and pepper.

2. Heat barbecue until hot and oil the grill bars. Place the chops on grill and sear one side for one minute, turn and brush with soy & honey marinade to glaze. Continue to turn at 2 minute intervals 4 or 5 times more until cooked to required degree. Take care not to overcook. Cooking time is from 10–15 minutes depending on thickness of chops and type of barbecue used.

3. Place apple rings on the grill bars a little after the chops commence cooking. Turn 2–3 times until soft and glazed. Place a piece of baking paper under the apples to prevent scorching. If cooking on a charcoal barbecue, use foil which has been brushed with oil.

4. Mix the chilli and cooked rice together and heat on the side of the barbecue in a foil or metal dish. Serve chops with chilli rice and garnish with glazed apple rings.

Serves 4-6

Hot Dogs with Mustard Relish

Ingredients

1kg/2¼lb frankfurters or thin sausages
1 cup barbecue sauce
12 hot dog rolls

mild mustard for serving
gherkin relish or tomato pickles to serve

Method

1. Heat the barbecue and oil the grill bars. Place frankfurters or sausages, turn to heat on the grill evenly, so the skin does not burst. Continue to cook for 10–12 minutes, brushing with a little barbecue sauce as they are turned. Push to cooler part of barbecue if cooking too quickly or turn down the heat.

2. Split the rolls, keeping the 2 halves attached and place cutside down on hot plate to toast.

3. Fill the roll with frankfurter or sausage, squeeze a row of mustard along the side and spoon in the gherkin relish or tomato pickle.

Perfect T-Bone Steak

**Many a time this delicious steak has been ruined on the barbecue.
Cook on all barbecues and improvise a hood if using a flattop barbecue.**

Ingredients

4 T-bone steaks
2 teaspoons crushed garlic
2 teaspoons oil
salt and pepper
Garlic Butter
55g/2oz butter

1 teaspoon crushed garlic
1 tablespoon parsley flakes
2 teaspoons lemon juice
**mix all ingredients together and
serve in a pot with a spoon**

Method

1. Bring the steaks to room temperate. Mix garlic, oil and salt and pepper together. Rub onto both sides of the steak. Stand for 10–15 minutes at room temperature.

2. Heat the barbecue until hot and oil the grill bars. Arrange the steaks and sear for one minute each side. Move steaks to cooler part of the barbecue to continue cooking over moderate heat, or turn heat down. If heat cannot be reduced then elevate on a wire cakerack placed on the grill bars. Cook until desired doneness is achieved. Total time 5–6 minutes for rare, 7–10 minutes for medium and 10–14 minutes for well done. Turn during cooking.

3. Serve on a heated steak plate and top with a dollop of garlic butter. Serve with jacket potatoes. See page 60

Serves 4

Ling Fish Fillets
with Lemon and Coriander

Ingredients

1 teaspoon chopped fresh ginger
1 teaspoon crushed garlic
2 tablespoons finely chopped coriander

2 tablespoon olive oil
1½ tablespoon lemon juice
455g/1lb Ling Fish fillets (4 portions)

Method

1. Mix the first 5 ingredients together in a shallow dish. Place the fillets in the dish and turn to coat well. Cover and stand 10–15 minutes.

2. Heat the barbecue to medium/hot and oil the grill bars. Place a sheet of baking paper over the bars and make a few slashes between the grill bars to allow ventilation. Place the fish on the paper and cook for 3–4 minutes each side according to thickness. Brush with marinade during cooking. Remove to plate. Heat any remaining marinade and pour over the fish.

3. Serve with Jacket Chats (page 56) and a salad

   Tip: Fish is cooked, if when tested with a fork, it flakes or the sections pull away. Red Snapper, Haddock and Perch may also be used.

   Serves 4

22

Skewered Chicken Liver
with Coriander

Cook on any flat-top barbecue or electric barbecue grill.

Ingredients

2 finely chopped coriander
1 teaspoon crushed garlic
1 teaspoon chopped
fresh ginger
2 teaspoons oil

1 tablespoon lemon juice
255g/9oz chicken livers
6 rashers bacon
toothpicks

Method

1. Place coriander, crushed garlic, chopped ginger oil and lemon juice in a bowl. Cut chicken livers into 2 through centre membrane and carefully stir into the coriander marinade. Cover and refrigerate for 1 hour or more.

2. Cut each bacon strip into 3 approximately 10cm/4in strips. Wrap a strip of bacon around each halved liver and secure with a toothpick.

3. Heat the barbecue until hot. Place on overturned wire cake-rack over the grill bars. Arrange the skewered livers on the rack. Cook for 8–10 minutes, turning frequently and brushing with any remaining marinade.

Serve as finger food.

Yield approximately 22 skewers.

Tandoori Chicken Kofta

Ingredients

Kofta
455g/1lb chicken mince
$^1/_2$ cup dried breadcrumbs
1 medium onion, finely chopped
1 tablespoon of chopped parsley
$^1/_2$ teaspoon salt
$^1/_4$ teaspoon pepper
Tandoori paste (page 89)

For Serving
1 cup thick yoghurt
2 tablespoons Tandoori paste
1 tablespoon lemon juice
100g/3$^1/_2$oz mixed salad greens

Method

1. Mix all the Kofta ingredients together and combine well by hand to distribute ingredients evenly and make the texture finer.

2. With wet hands, shape tablespoons of mixture into sausage shapes and flatten slightly.

3. Heat the barbecue to medium-high and oil the grill bars or hotplate. Place on the Koftas on the grill and cook for 15 minutes, turning frequently. Brush with a little oil as they cook if needed.

4. Mix together the yoghurt, tandoori paste and lemon juice.

5. When Koftas are cooked, transfer to a platter lined with salad greens. Drizzle with yoghurt sauce or serve the sauce in a bowl on the platter.

Serves 6

Deluxe Hamburgers

Ingredients

Buns and suggested fillings
14 hamburger buns
softened butter for spreading
1 lettuce, separated into leaves,
washed and drained
1 bunch rocket, washed & drained
2 large onions, thinly sliced and
cooked on the hotplate
sandwich cheese slices
1 bottle tomato sauce/ ketchup
1 jar vegetable relish of
your choice

Burger Patties
1kg/2^1/$_4$lb beef mince
1 large onion, grated or
processed
^{1}/$_2$ cup dried breadcrumbs
^{1}/$_2$ teaspoon salt
^{1}/$_4$ teaspoon pepper
3 tablespoons barbecue
or tomato sauce
2 tablespoons water

Method

1. Combine all the ingredients for the burger patties, knead by hand to distribute evenly and make the texture finer. Rest for 20 minutes in the refrigerator. With wet hands, shape into 14 flat patties about 8cm/3 in in diameter.

2. Heat barbecue to hot, oil the grill bars, place on the patties and cook for 5–6 minutes on each side, brush with a little oil as they cook.

3. Split the buns and lightly spread with softened butter. Place buttered side down on hotplate and toast to golden colour.

To Assemble: Place a lettuce leaf on bottom half of bun, top with cooked patty, tomato sauce, onions, cheese slice, rocket leaf and your choice of pickle or relish. Top with remaining bun.

Have fun around the barbecue while creating a deluxe hamburger.

Serves 14

Quick Sesame Chicken Wings

Ingredients

2kg/4½lb chicken wings, tips removed

1 quantity soy and honey marinade (page 90)

3 tablespoons sesame seeds, toasted

Method

1. Place wings in a large container and smother with the marinade. Cover and marinade for 30 minutes at room temperature or longer in the refrigerator.

2. Place half the wings in a microwave-safe dish and microwave for 10 minutes on high. Remove and microwave the remainder.

3. Heat the barbecue until hot. Place a wire cake-rack over the grill bars and place the wings on the rack. Brush with marinade left in the bow. Turn and brush the wings frequently until they are brown and crisp.

4. Spread sesame seeds on a foil tray and place on the barbecue. Shake occasionally as they toast. Sprinkle over the browned chicken wings.

   Serve as finger food.

Lamb and Salsa Pockets

Ingredients

$^1/_2$ leg of lamb
1 tablespoon lemon juice
salt and pepper
2 teaspoons oil
1 teaspoon crushed garlic

bamboo skewers, soaked
300g/10$^1/_2$oz tomato salsa
6 pack pocket bread
3 cups shredded lettuce

Method

1. Cut lamb into 1cm/$^1/_2$ in cubes. Place in a bowl and add lemon juice, salt, pepper, oil and garlic. Cover and marinate at room temperature for 20 minutes. Thread onto skewers.

2. Heat the barbecue and oil the grill bars. Place the salsa into a foil or metal container and place at side of barbecue to heat a little.

3. Cook lamb skewers for 3–4 minutes each side. Halve the pocket bread and heat a little on the barbecue. Open the pocket, fill with lettuce, lamb (skewer removed) and top with heated salsa.

Serve immediately.

Serves 6

Glazed Banana and Bacon Bites

Serve as a starter to a barbecue meal or serve to accompany barbecue steaks.

Ingredients

2 or 3 large firm, bananas
4 rashers streaky bacon

honey & chilli marinade
(page 89)

Method

1. Peel the bananas and cut into 3cm/1in thick slices at an angle. Cut bacon into 10cm/4in long strips and wrap around each piece of banana. Secure with a toothpick and brush with honey marinade.

2. Place a wire cake-rack over the grill or hotplate of the heated barbecue. Arrange the banana and bacon bites on the rack. Cook for 10 minutes, brushing with marinade and turning frequently.

28

Teriyaki Prawns

Ingredients

1kg/2¼lb fresh green prawns in shell, normal or king

teriyaki marinade (page 89)
bamboo skewers, soaked

Method

1. Shell the prawns, leaving the tails intact. Place in a non-metal dish and smother with the marinade. Cover and refrigerate for 1–2 hours. Thread onto soaked skewers. For small prawns thread 2–3 per skewer: for king prawns thread only one from tail-end to top.

2. Heat the barbecue and place a square of baking paper on the grill bars. Place the prawns on the grill brushing with marinade on both sides as they cook. Cook until prawns turn pink in colour. Take care not to overcook.

Yield 10

the medium
cook

This section features recipes for thicker cuts that require from 20 to 30 minutes to cook. So you need to get started a little earlier to cook the barbecue.

Foods in this section are cooked over both indirect and direct heat at a lower temperature. The thicker cuts need longer for the heat to penetrate and cook through to the centre without burning the outside. Kettle barbecues and hooded barbecues, either charcoal or gas which provide both direct and indirect heat are very suitable. Flat-top barbecues are also used, with some adjustments to techniques. Electric barbecue grills with hoods may also be used. The smaller table grills are suitable for some recipes.

Capsicum -Barbecued Whole Snapper with Gherkin Mayonnaise Relish

1 whole snapper (1 1/2kg/3 1/3lb)
3 tablespoons of chopped
red capsicum (bell pepper)
2 teaspoons chopped fresh basil
2 tablespoons lemon juice
1 tablespoon olive oil

Gherkin Mayonnaise
1 cup mayonnaise
1/3 cup gherkin relish
or chopped gherkins

Method

1. Cut and scale the fish and rinse well. Pat dry with paper towels.

2. Mix the capsicum (bell pepper), basil, lemon juice and oil together. Spoon some into the cavity and spread the remainder over the fish.

3. Lay the fish on a large sheet of oiled foil and roll up the edges to form an enclosure around the fish, leaving the top of the fish exposed (except for flat-top).

   Charcoal Kettle and Hooded Gas Barbecue – Place the fish on the grill bars, indirect heat. Cover with lid or hood and cook for 35–40 minutes or until fish flakes when tested with a fork.

   Flat Top Charcoal or Gas Barbecue – Prepare fish as above and cover completely with foil. Place on a wire rack and place the rack on top of the grill bars, elevating so that the fish is 10cm/4 in above the source of heat. Cook for 10–12 minutes each side. Turn carefully using a large spatula or place fish in a hinged fish rack and turn when needed.

   Electric Barbecue Grill – Prepare as for kettle, elevate on a wire rack place on the grill bars. Set barbecue to medium high. Cover with hood and cook 25–35 minutes.

   Gherkin Mayonnaise: Mix mayonnaise and gherkin relish or chopped gerkin together.

   Serve fish while hot with gherkin mayonnaise and accompany with potato wedges and salad.

   Serves 4

Glazed Pork Spare Ribs

May be cooked on all barbecues using direct heat.

Ingredients

1kg/2$^{1}/_{4}$lb pork spare ribs (American-Style)	**soy and honey marinade (page 90)**

Method

1. Place spare ribs on a large sheet of heavy-duty foil and cover both sides generously with marinade. Wrap into a double-folded parcel, making sure all joins are well-sealed to prevent leakage. Stand for at least half an hour before cooking. Place in refrigerator if not to be cooked immediately.

2. Prepare the barbecue for direct-heat cooking. Place a wire cake-rack on the grill bars to stand 2$^{1}/_{2}$ cm/1 in above the bars. Place ribs in the foil parcel on the rack and cook for 10 minutes each side.

3. Remove to a plate, remove ribs and discard foil, then return ribs to rack. Continue cooking brushing with fresh sauce or marinade and turning each minute until ribs are well browned and crisp (about 10 minutes). Total cooking time is approximately 30–35 minutes.

Serves 4

Note: Ribs may be cooked by indirect heat in a hooded barbecue. There is no need to wrap in foil. Place over indirect heat after marinating. Brush and turn frequently with lid down for 1 hour or more. Cooking in the foil over direct heat cuts cooking time in half.

Hawaiian Pork Kebabs

Ingredients

1kg/2¼lb boneless pork cut into
2½cm/1 in cubes
soy and honey marinade
(page 90)
½ pineapple cut into
2½cm/1in cubes

2 red capsicums (bell peppers)
cut into 2cm/1in squares
1 small onion cut into 4 and
separated
bamboo skewers, soaked,
or metal skewers

Method

1. Place pork cubes in a non-metal container and stir in enough sauce to coat well. Cover and marinate for 30 minutes at room temperature, or longer in refrigerator.

2. Thread pork cubes onto skewers alternately with the pineapple, capsicum (bell pepper) and onion pieces. Brush with marinade and cook according to barbecue type, below.

   Charcoal Kettle and Hooded Gas Barbecue – Prepare barbecue for indirect heat. Place on oiled grill bars and brush well with marinade. Cook with lid or hood down for 25/30 minutes, turn once or twice and brush with marinade.

   Flat-top and Electric Barbecue Grill – Place a wire cake-rack to sit 2½ cm/1 in over the grill bars. Heat barbecue until hot. Place the kebabs on grill and brush with marinade. Turn after 5 minutes and brush again. Continue to cook for a total time of approximately 25 minutes.

Honey -Glazed Thick Straight Sausages

Ingredients

The advantage of cooking straight sausages is that they will have all-around, even contact with the grill bars or hotplate to evenly cook. When they curl, the even contact is difficult. So thread onto skewers to prevent the curl.

2kg/4^1/$_2$lb thick pork or beef sausages   **metal or bamboo skewers**

honey & chilli marinade (page 89)

Method

1. Smooth each sausage out straight and carefully push skewer through centre end-to-end. Don't go off centre or the sausage will curl. If using long metal skewers, thread 2 sausages.

2. Heat barbecue to normal for indirect heat and medium for direct heat. Grease the grill bars or hotplate and arrange sausages on the grill. Roll the sausages back and forth to gradually heat all sides evenly until there is a colour change. This gradually expands the skin and sausages will not burst.

3. Continue as follows:

   Kettle or Hooded Barbecue – Place over indirect heat and brush with marinade. Cover with lid and cook for 20–25 minutes. Brush with marinade on all sides 3 more times during cooking. Remove skewers for final cooking.

   Flat-top Gas – Place a sheet of baking paper under sausages, brush with marinade and turn frequently. Cook for 20–25 minutes until well glazed and cooked through. Remove skewers for final cooking.

   Electric Barbecue Grills – As for flat-top

   Serves 4 to 8

Mexican Sausages

Ingredients

1kg/2¼lb glazed straight
sausages
(page 35)
2 small packets (55g/2oz) corn
chips, lightly crushed

1 jar tomato salsa
100g/3½oz grated tasty cheddar
cheese

Method

1. Cook sausages as directed on page 35. When cooked, slit each sausage almost through. Open slit and sprinkle in some of the corn chip pieces, spoon in a generous amount of salsa and top with grated cheese. Return to the barbecue grill plate. Prop up so as not to spill filling.

2. Cover with lid or hood and cook until cheese melts, about 1 minute. If using a flat-top or electric barbecue grill, improvise a cover by using a large saucepan lid or overturned baking dish to enclose heat so cheese can melt.

Serves 8

Mini Lamb Roast with Barbecued Noodles

Ingredients

1 trim lamb mini roast
2 tablespoons chopped
fresh coriander
1 teaspoon crushed garlic
1 tablespoon lemon juice
salt, pepper
1 tablespoon oil

Barbecued Noodles
1 tablespoon chopped
fresh coriander
100g/3½oz Fetta cheese,
crumbled
1 teaspoon crushed garlic
½ teaspoon chopped chilli
(optional)
455g/1lb Hokkien noodles

Method

1. Tie the mini roast with kitchen string to give it a higher shape. The roast has a half moon shape and the outer edges will dry if roast is not tied.

2. In a glass bowl, mix remaining ingredients together. Drop in the lamb and turn to coat on all sides. Marinate for 1 hour at room temperature, or longer in the refrigerator.

3. Cook as follows:

   Kettle or Hooded Gas Barbecue – Prepare barbecue for indirect heat. Place lamb over drip tray in centre of barbecue to use indirect heat, cover with lid or hood and cook for 35–40 minutes. There is no need to turn. Or, place lamb in foil tray in same position on rack so cooking juices will be retained. Brush with marinade as it cooks and turn once or twice.

Barbecued Noodles:

1. Rinse noodles in hot water and separate. Drain very well.
   Mix coriander, Fetta, garlic and chilli to a paste.
2. Heat the barbecue hotplate or use a tin baking dish on grill plate. Oil hot plate or dish, add the noodles and toss around while adding the coriander paste. Mix well and heat through.
3. Place on serving plate or platter.
4. Slice lamb and arrange over noodles. Drizzle withr any remaining pan juices.

Mustard and Honey Chicken Drumsticks with Mustard Cream Sauce

Ingredients

2kg/4$^{1}/_{2}$lb chicken drumsticks (medium-size)
1$^{1}/_{2}$ cups honey and chilli marinade (page 90)

Mustard Cream Sauce
300ml/10$^{1}/_{2}$oz carton sour cream
1 cup Dijon mustard
$^{1}/_{2}$ cup honey and chilli marinade (page 90)

Method

1. Place drumsticks in a non-metal container and pour enough marinade over to coat well. Cover and stand 30 minutes at room temperature or longer in the refrigerator.

2. To cook, prepare barbecue as follows:

   Kettle and Hooded Barbecues –Heat until hot, place drumsticks over indirect heat and cover with lid or hood. Cook for 15 minutes. Remove hood, turn drumsticks and brush with marinade every 8 minutes, replacing hood until cooked approximately 45 minutes cooking time. Continue turning and brushing with marinade as above 3 more times at 8 minute intervals or until drumsticks are cooked through to the bone. Total cooking time 40–45 minutes.

   Flat-top, Charcoal and Gas Barbecues –Heat the barbecue until hot. Place a wire cake-rack over the grill bars and oil the rack. The rack should stand 2$^{1}/_{2}$ cm/1in above the bars. Place the drumsticks on the rack and cook for 15–20 minutes, turning frequently. Place a square of baking paper onto the grill bars. Transfer the drumsticks onto the baking paper. Brush with marinade and turn frequently. Cook for a further 10–15 minutes until well glazed and cooked to the bone.

   Mustard Cream Sauce: Mix the sour cream, mustard, honey & chilli marinade together in a heat-proof bowl. Place at the side of the barbecue to heat through. Serve drumsticks with the mustard cream sauce and vegetable accompaniments or salad.

   Serves 6/10

Pesto Crusted Racks of Lamb with Tomatoes and Basil Bruschettes

For best results, prepare the lamb the night before.

Ingredients

**4 to 6 racks lamb,
3 to 4 cutlets on each
3 cups soft, white
breadcrumbs
¼ cup pinenuts
3 tablespoons fresh
chopped basil**

**1 teaspoon crushed garlic
2 tablespoons grated
Romano
or Parmesan cheese
1 tablespoon lemon juice
1 small egg (55g/2oz),
lightly beaten**

Basil Tomatoes
**cherry tomatoes
2 tablespoons fresh
basil, chopped**

Basil Bruschettes
**Turkish bread
200g/7oz ricotta cheese
2 tablespoons fresh basil,
chopped**

Method

1. Trim some of the fat from the racks, leaving a thin layer. Rub all over with a little crushed garlic. Mix remaining ingredients together to form a damp mixture. Pack onto each rack, patting down well. Place racks onto a flat tray, cover with plastic wrap and refrigerate.

2. Cook as directed below and serve with basil tomatoes and Bruschettes. Serve 2–3 cutlets per serve. (Not suitable for flat-top barbecue)

Kettle Barbecue, Hooded Gas Barbecue –Prepare barbecue for indirect heat. Place racks of lamb on the oiled grill bars, over the drip pan, in an upright position. Place in pairs, back-to-back for support. Cover with lid or hood and cook for 35–45 minutes. Remove from barbecue. Cover with foil and rest 5 minutes before serving.

Basil Tomatoes: Cross-cut the top of cherry tomatoes (larger size) and place a drop of chopped basil on top. Sit in foil tray, cover with foil and cook 10 minutes on side of barbecue.

Basil Bruschettes: Slice Turkish bread into 1½ cm/½in slices. Mix 200g/7oz ricotta cheese, with two tablespoons chopped basil. Spread onto the bread slices. Place on barbecue, cheese-side up and cook base for 2 minutes to toast. Place a piece of baking paper on grill bars and turn cheese-side down onto the paper. Cook 1 to 2 minutes until cheese has coloured slightly and grill-bar markings are defined.

Piquant Pork Fillets with Polenta

4 pork fillets (300g/10oz each)
170g/6oz jar sun-dried tomato pesto
1 tablespoon chopped basil

2 tablespoons lemon juice
1 tablespoon olive oil
1 quantity polenta (see page 64)

Method

1. To make marinade: mix together sun-dried tomato pesto, chopped basil, lemon juice and olive oil.

2. Carefully remove the silvery white membrane from the top of the fillets with a sharp pointed knife. Place fillets in a suitable container and cover both sides with half of the marinade, (reserving remainder). Cover and marinate for 30 minutes at room temperature, or longer in the refrigerator.

3. Cook as follows:

Charcoal Kettle or Hooded Gas Barbecue —Prepare barbecue for indirect cooking. Place the fillets on oiled grill bars over the drip tray. Cook with lid on for 40 minutes. Brush twice with some of the remaining capsicum (bell pepper) mixture used for marinade. When fillets are almost cooked, cut prepared polenta into 10 x 7cm/4 x 3in slabs, remove from dish and brush with oil. Place over direct heat and cook for 4 minutes on each side until golden.

Flat-top and Electric Barbecue Grills —Heat until hot. Place a wire cake-rack to stand 2$\frac{1}{2}$cm/1in above grill bars. Place fillets on cake-rack and cook for approximately 20 minutes each side. Brushing with marinade when turned. Cut polenta as above and cook on oiled grill bars 5 minutes on each side.

To serve: Slice the fillets into 2$\frac{1}{2}$cm/1in thick diagonal slices. Overlap onto the polenta slice and top with the reserved and warmed tomato mixture.

Serve with suitable vegetables.

Serves 4/6

Tandoori Chicken Halves

For best results cook in a kettle barbecue using charcoal.

Ingredients

2 x No. 8 fresh chickens
1 x quantity tandoori paste
(page 89)
¹/₄ cup lemon juice

endive leaves for serving
tomato and chilli pickle
for serving

Method

1. Split chicken in half, cutting through the breast bone and back bone with a cleaver or large, sharp knife. Place cut-side down on a board and press down the breast to flatten with the heel of your hand. Place in a non-metal, wide container. Prepare the tandoori paste and rub all over the chicken. Cover and marinate several hours in the refrigerator.

2. Heat the barbecue and place chicken on grill bars over the drip tray, indirect heat, skin-side up. Cook with lid on for 40–45 minutes. Baste occasionally with any left-over tandoori mixture.

3. Serve on a bed of endive. Accompany with tomato and chilli pickle, or other of your choice.

Serves 6

the long
cook

Keep your kitchen cool in summer by cooking roasts and festive turkey and hams outdoors on the barbecue.

The Long Cook deals with foods which take 45 minutes to 2 hours or more to cook. Kettle or hooded barbecues produce the sought after smokey flavour, and the addition of different wood will give added interest. The enclosed space keeps the meat moist and tender, and it is far easier to baste and glaze with the delicious marinade flavours.

Electric hooded barbecue grills may be used outdoors on the patio or verandah. Whichever you use, the big advantage is keeping the kitchen cool in summer.

Barbecued Butterflied Leg of Lamb with Pickle-topped Potatoes

Ingredients

1 boned leg of lamb
1 teaspoon crushed garlic
1 teaspoon freshly chopped ginger
2 tablespoons Dijon mustard

2 teaspoons olive oil
salt, pepper
12 jacket potatoes (see page 60)
255g/9oz jar tomato
and chilli pickle

Method

1. Ask your butcher to bone the lamb leg. Place skin-side down on a chopping board and open out. Cut into all the thicker parts of the meat at a 45° angle until almost through and open out (butterfly). Beat the open areas with a meat mallet to flatten to an even thickness, about 3cm/1in thick.

2. Mix the garlic, ginger, mustard, oil, salt and pepper together and spread over the surface of the lamb. Fold the 2 sides and the shank end over to meet in the centre, making a flat roast. Pass 2 long metal skewers through diagonally from opposite corners, weaving to secure the folded pieces, and if necessary, use small skewers to secure other parts. These will also keep the lamb flat while cooking. Stand 30 minutes at room temperature before cooking or refrigerate until needed. Before cooking return to room temperature.

3. Oil the outside of the lamb and oil the grill bars or hot plate and cook as follows:

   Charcoal Kettle or Gas Hooded Barbecue – Prepare a normal fire or place on medium gas grill bars over the drip tray, indirect heat. Place foil-wrapped potatoes around the lamb. Cook for 50–60 minutes turning once.

   Electric Barbecue Grill with Hood – Place a wire cake-rack on the grill bars to stand 2½cm/1in above the bars. Place the lamb on the rack and cover with the hood. Cook for 45 minutes, then increase the heat to high for a further 10 minutes. Turn once.

   Flat Top Barbecue – Heat the hotplate to medium and oil it well. Cook for 20 minutes on each side and a further 5 minutes each side until done.

4. Rest the lamb covered in foil for 10 minutes. Cut into slices and serve with the potatoes and salad.

Pickle-topped Potatoes

Test potatoes with a skewer before removing from barbecue. Remove foil, cut a deep cross in the top and push with fingers at the base to open out the top. Spoon a teaspoonful of tomato pickle on top and serve with the lamb.

Serves 6

Barbecued Chicken and Potatoes

Ingredients

No. 18 or 20 fresh chicken

1 cup barbecue sauce

1kg/2^{1}/$_{4}$lb potatoes, washed, peeled and cut into pieces

1 tablespoon lemon juice

1 teaspoon crushed garlic

5 small pickling onions

^{1}/$_{4}$ cup water

2 tablespoons oil

Method

1. Wash chicken inside and out, making sure any remaining giblets in the cavity are scraped out. Rinse cavity well, stand upright to drain and pat dry with paper towels. Brush the chicken inside and out with barbecue sauce. Place the chicken in the centre of a large foil baking dish and surround with prepared potatoes and onions. Mix lemon juice, garlic, salt, pepper, water and oil together and pour over the potatoes.

2. Cook as follows:

   Kettle or Hooded Gas Barbecue —Prepare for normal fire or medium-high, indirect heat. Place the tray containing chicken and potatoes on the grill bars over indirect heat. Cover with lid and cook for 50 minutes. Turn potatoes and brush chicken with barbecue sauce. Continue to brush chicken every 10 minutes for total cooking time of 1^{1}/$_{4}$ to 1^{1}/$_{2}$ hours. Chicken is done if juices run clear when pricked with a skewer. Stand 10 minutes before carving. Remove potatoes from tray when cooked. May be browned over direct heat if needed.

   Electric Barbecue Grill with Hood — Place dish containing chicken and potatoes on a wire cake-rack standing 2^{1}/$_{2}$ cm/1 in above the grill bars. Cook on medium-high as directed above.

Serves 8

Barbecued Leg of Lamb in Paper

Ingredients

2kg/4 1/2lb leg of lamb
2 teaspoons salt
1 teaspoon pepper
1/2 cup lemon juice
2 tblspns freshy crushed garlic
Romano or Parmesan cheese
cut into 8 x 1/2 cm/1/5in cubes

170g/6oz jar sun-dried tomato
pesto
2 sheets greaseproof paper, oiled
1 sheet brown paper,
oiled on both sides

Method

1. Wash the lamb and pat dry. Make about 8 incisions on each side of the lamb with the point of a small knife. Place lamb in a suitable non-corrosive dish, rub all over with salt and pepper and pour over the lemon juice, allowing the juice to enter the incisions. Stand 30 minutes. Push a 1/2 teaspoon of crushed garlic into each incision followed by a cheese cube. Rub all over with tomato pesto. Wrap the lamb in the 2 sheets of oiled greaseproof paper and then wrap into a parcel with the brown paper. Tie with kitchen string.

2. Prepare Kettle or Gas Hooded Barbecue for indirect heat on medium-high. Place the lamb parcel onto oiled grill bars over the drip tray and cook, indirect heat, for 2 hours. Turn lamb after 1 hour. When cooked, remove from barbecue and rest for 20 minutes before removing from paper and carving. Take care when opening parcel, that any juices are collected in a bowl. Reheat juices and serve with the carved meat.

3. Serve with a mild mustard, a green salad and garlic bread.

Serves 6 to 8

Glazed Scotch Fillet Roast with Tomato Potato Wedges

Ingredients

1 ½ kg/3 ⅓ lb whole piece of scotch fillet	2 tablespoons sun-dried tomato pesto
salt, pepper	1 tablespoon water
2 teaspoons oil	1 tablespoon olive oil
5 medium-sized potatoes	herbed wine marinade
1 teaspoon crushed garlic	(page 89)

Method

1. Rub the salt, pepper and oil all over the roast and tie with kitchen string at 2½ cm/1 in intervals, to keep in shape.

2. Peel and halve the potatoes then cut each half into 4–6 wedges. Rinse potato wedges well, drain and place in a large bowl. Mix garlic, tomato pesto, water and oil together, pour over wedges and turn to coat well. Place in a large foil dish, in a single layer if possible.

3 Cook as follows:

   Kettle and Gas Hooded Barbecue –Prepare charcoal barbecue for normal heat and set gas barbecue to medium-high. Arrange both for indirect cooking. Place the roast over the drip tray, cover with lid or hood and cook for 45 minutes without turning. Proceed to brush with herbed wine marinade every 10 minutes to complete 75 minutes for rare, and 90 minutes for medium. Place potatoes over direct heat for the last 40 minutes of cooking (when you first commence brushing with marinade). Turn wedges over after 20 minutes.

   Electric Barbecue Grills – Preheat to medium-high and place a wire cake-rack to stand 2½ cm/1 in above the grill bars. Place roast in a foil baking dish. Cover with the hood and cook for 40 minutes. Proceed as instructed for kettle and gas barbecues. Place wedges on the hot plate for 40 minutes, turning after 20 minutes.

3. Stand roast covered with foil for 10 minutes before carving. Carve and serve with tomato potato wedges and vegetables or salad of choice.

   Serves 8 to 10

Loin of Pork with Sun-dried Tomato and Apple Stuffing

Ingredients

1 ¹/₂ kg/3 ¹/₃lb boned loin of park with flap on and rind removed
1 tablespoon sun-dried tomato pesto
1 tablespoon honey & chilli marinade (page 89)

Sun-dried Tomato and Apple Stuffing
1 cup soft white, breadcrumbs
2 tablespoons sun-dried tomato pesto
1 red apple, finely diced
1 tablespoon honey & chilli marinade (page 89)
salt, pepper

Method

1. It is best to order the loin of pork, with the flap on, 2 days in advance as it is not usually included.

2. Score the fat layer in a diamond pattern with a pointed knife. Mix stuffing ingredients together and place along the roast, packing it up against the loin meat. Roll the flap over tightly; fasten with skewers while the roast is tied with kitchen string at 2¹/₂cm/1 in intervals. Remove the skewers.

3. Rub the sun-dried tomato pesto over the surface of the rolled roast. Cook as follows:

   Kettle and Hooded Gas Barbecue – Prepare barbecue for indirect heat, normal or medium heat. Place the rolled loin over the drip pan, indirect heat, cover with lid or hood and cook for 50 minutes. Commence glazing with marinade every 10 minutes for a further 45–55 minutes; total cooking time is approximately 1¹/₄–1³/₄ hours. If using a meat thermometer, inside temperature should reach 75°C–77°C/167°F–171°F.

   Electric Barbecue Grill with Hood – Set temperature to medium high or Hood range. Place roast in a foil pan and stand on a wire cake-rack to come 2¹/₂ cm/1 in above grill bars. Cover with hood and cook as above.

4. When cooked, wrap foil and stand 15 minutes before carving. Slice the roast and serve garnished with small stuffed apples (page 86) and vegetables of choice.

Serves 8 to 10

Marinated Bolar Beef
with Apple and Chilli Stuffing

Long marinating tenderises the bolar roast.

Ingredients

**2kg/4¹/₂lb bolar beef roast
teriyaki marinade (page 89)**
Stuffing
**1 tablespoon butter
1 small onion, thinly sliced**

**2 rashers bacon, rind
removed and chopped
¹/₂ teaspoons freshly chopped
red chilli
1 cooking apple, diced (skin on)**

Method

1. Cut a pocket, slanting downwards, in the bolar roast. Place in a suitable non-metal container and smother generously with the marinade. Cover and refrigerate for 24 hours.

2. **Prepare the stuffing** —Heat butter in a small pan, add onion and bacon and fry for a few minutes, then add the chilli and apple. Stir well and continue to cook for 3 minutes. Allow to cool. Remove the roast from the marinade and pat dry. Place the stuffing in the pocket and close with a skewer or tie roast with kitchen string.

3. Cook as follows:

   Kettle or Hooded Gas Barbecue -Prepare for indirect heat, medium-high. Place roast on oiled grill bars over the drip tray. Cover with lid or hood and cook for 50 minutes. Lift lid and brush with marinade and continue to brush with marinade every 15 minutes for a total cooking time of 1¹/₂–2 hours. Rest the roast, wrapped in foil, for 15 minutes before carving. Carve and serve the roast with vegetables. (See page 55 to 65)

   Electric Barbecue Grills with Hood- Heat to medium-high. Place a wire cake-rack to stand 2¹/₂ cm/1 in above grill bars. Place the roast in a foil baking tray and cook as above.

Outdoor Christmas Turkey

Ingredients

Ingredients

4–5kg/9–12lb turkey
salt, pepper
red wine & garlic marinade
(page 90)
Stuffing
2 rashers bacon, finely chopped
I onion, finely chopped

4 cups/240g/8oz fresh breadcrumbs
2 tablespoons red wine
& garlic marinade (page 90)
I egg
I tablespoon sultanas or
chopped dried apricots

Method

1. Wash turkey inside and out, scraping out any remaining giblets. Rinse cavity well, drain and pat dry with paper towels. Sprinkle salt and pepper inside the cavity and brush the outside with the marinade.

2. Cook as follows:

   Kettle or Gas Hooded Barbecue – Prepare barbecue for indirect cooking and heat to medium-high. Place turkey on the oiled grill bars over the drip tray (use a large one or add a second tray). Cover and cook for one hour. Uncover and brush with marinade. Place foil strips on each side of turkey, if necessary, to prevent scorching in charcoal barbecue. Cover and cook I to I ½ hours more, brushing with marinade every 20 minutes.

2. Prepare stuffing when turkey is first placed on barbecue. Fry the bacon in a heated pan until fat runs. Add onion and cook until soft, then mix both into the breadcrumbs with remaining ingredients. Spoon into greased muffin pan or individual foil cups. Cook over direct heat for 20 minutes.

3. When turkey is cooked, cover and rest for 20 minutes before carving. Vegetables may be cooked during this time. Skim the fat from juices in the drip tray. Stir in a little marinade, reheat and serve for gravy.

Stuffed Turkey Breast Roll

Ingredients

I turkey breast, approx I¹/₃kg/3lb
salt, pepper
¹/₂ cup red wine & garlic marinade (page 90)
Stuffing
I medium onion, finely chopped
2 cups fresh breadcrumbs

145g/5oz shaved ham, chopped
2 tablespoons finely chopped parsley
2 tablespoons red wine & garlic marinade (page 90)

Method

1. Make a cut into the thick part of the breast, slanting the knife at a 45° angle and cutting almost through. Open out and pound the area with the side of a meat mallet to thin out evenly, then rub with salt and pepper. Mix the stuffing ingredients together and place along the centre of the length. Form into a roll and secure with skewers. Tie with kitchen string at 2¹/₂ cm/I in intervals then remove the skewers.

2. Cook as follows:

   Kettle and Gas Hooded Barbecue –Prepare barbecue for indirect heat, medium-high. Oil the grill bars and place turkey roll over the drip tray. Cover with lid or hood and cook 20 minutes, brushing with marinade every 15 minutes until cooked when tested. Juices will run clear when pierced with a skewer. Total cooking time approximately one hour.

   Electric Barbecue Grill with Hood –Preheat to roast temperature. Place turkey roll in a foil dish and stand on a rack placed on the grill bars. Cover with hood and cook as above.

2. Stand the turkey roll 10 minutes before carving. Serve with glazed sweet potato and jacket potatoes (see 60). Mix pan juices with a little marinade and serve as gravy.

Serves 6

Standing Rib Roast
with Cajun Potato Cakes and Chunky Salsa

Ingredients

1½kg/3⅓lb standing rib roast of beef
salt, pepper
2 teaspoons crushed garlic
2 tablespoons flour
300g/10½oz jar tomato salsa

Cajun Potato Cakes
4 medium-sized potatoes, boiled in their jackets
2 x 55g/2oz eggs, lightly beaten
2 teaspoons cajun seasoning
2 tablespoons olive oil
2 tablespoons flour
½ teaspoon salt

Method

1. Rub the roast with salt, pepper and crushed garlic and stand at room temperature for 20 minutes. Just before placing on the barbecue, dust all over with flour. This helps to seal in the juices. Place salsa in a small saucepan ready for heating and prepare potato cake mixture and

2. Cook as follows:

   Kettle and Gas Hooded Barbecue – Prepare to medium-high heat for indirect cooking. Stand roast on oiled grill bars over drip tray. Cover with lid or hood and cook for 1–1½ hours or until meat thermometer reaches 65° C–70°C/149°F–58°F. Remove from barbecue cover with foil and stand 20 minutes before carving.

   Electric Barbecue Grill – Preheat to medium-high. Stand roast in a foil baking dish. Place a wire cake-rack to stand 2½ cm/1in above the grill bars and set the roast. Cover with hood and cook as above.

   Cajun Potato Cakes – Skin the boiled potatoes and mash well. Add eggs, Cajun seasoning, olive oil, flour and salt. Mix well and form into 16 patties with floured hands. Cook on oiled hotplate or grill bars over direct heat for about 5 minutes on each side. Heat the salsa while patties are cooking. Carve the roast and serve with the Cajun potato cakes and salsa. Serves 8

Chinese Spiced Lamb

Ingredients

4 trim lamb topside steaks
115g/4oz mushrooms, sliced
2 medium zucchinis (courgettes), thinly sliced lenghwise
1 punnet cherry tomatoes, halved
2 sticks celery, thinly sliced
1 red capsicum (bell pepper), sliced

2 tablespoons honey
1 teaspoon Chinese five spice powder
1 teaspoon freshly chopped ginger
1 teaspoon freshly crushed garlic
crusty wholemeal bread

Method

1. Pre-heat barbecue to medium high.

2. Trim steaks of excess fat. Toss together mushrooms, zucchini (courgette), cherry tomatoes, celery and capsicum (bell pepper) in a salad bowl and refrigerate until required.

3. In a small bowl combine honey, five-spice powder, ginger and garlic.

4. Barbecue steaks 4–5 minutes each side. Cook a further 5 minutes, brushing with honey mixture and turning occasionally. Serve steaks with zucchini (courgette) salad and crusty bread Serves 4

barbecued
vegetables

Crunchy vegetables with a distinctive smoky barbecue flavour are an change from normal vegetable cooking. When you light up the barbie, make vegetables part of the menu. The addition of flavour-some ingredients makes them the main event.

Cooking vegetables on the barbecue can be done in many ways. They may be placed directly on the hotplate or grill bars or in foil trays. They may be cooked over direct or indirect heat. Vegetables are best cooked on the cooler part of the barbecue. For foil parcel cooking, elevate a few centimetres off the hotplate by placing on a wire cake-rack.

Barbecue Vegetable Toss

Ingredients

¹/₂ bunch shallots, trimmed and cut into 2cm/³/₄ in lengths	I small sweet potato, thinly sliced
I medium carrot, thinly sliced	¹/₂ chinese cabbage, roughly chopped
145g/5oz cauliflower florets	I cup teriyaki marinade (page 89)
115g/4oz snow peas (mangetout), trimmed	

Method

1. Heat the barbecue hotplate to medium high and oil well. Prepare vegetables and mix together. Pile onto the barbecue and spread out using tongs.

2. Place the cup of marinade in a metal container to heat through, which will make it flow more easily. Toss and cook the vegetables until they soften, then splash over the marinade whilst they complete cooking.

3. Remove to a pre-warmed serving dish while still a little crispy. Serve immediately with barbecued meats.

   Note: Other vegetable combinations may be used according to preference.

Chat Potatoes

Ingredients

255g/9oz chat potatoes, washed	2 tablespoons sweet mustard pickles
I tablespoon oil	foil to wrap
I teaspoon salt	

Method

1. Choose medium-sized chat potatoes for quick cooking. Place washed potatoes in a bowl and drizzle over the oil and salt, stirring to coat. Wrap each potato in a piece of foil. Place on the barbecue hot plate or grill bars as soon as you light the barbecue and before it is hot enough to cook the meat. This will give the potatoe a head start. Turn potatoes every few minutes. After barbecue heats and meats are being cooked, turn potatoes more frequently. Test with a skewer if soft, remove and set aside. Potatoes will take about 15–20 minutes according to size and degree of heat.

2. Unwrap potatoes, leaving foil at potato base. Cut a cross in the top and squeeze the base to open out. Spoon mustard pickle in centre and serve immediately.

Serves 4

Eggplant (aubergine) Stacks

Ingredients

2 or 3 large eggplants (aubergine)   6 to 8 slices Cheddar
$^1/_2$ cup olive oil   or Mozzarella cheese
300g/10$^1/_2$oz jar tomato salsa

Method

1. Slice eggplant (aubergine) lengthwise into 1cm/$^1/_2$in thick slices.

2. Heat the barbecue grill and hot plate to medium-high and oil well. Brush eggplant with oil and place on barbecue. Cook about 4 minutes on each side until rosy brown. Place the salsa in a small container on side of barbecue. As eggplants (aubergine) cook, spread one slice with salsa topped with second slice of eggplant (audergine. Spread again with salsa and place a cheese slice on top. Cover with lid or hood and cook until cheese just begins to melt and encases the stack. If cooking on a flattop, use a suitable saucepan lid or baking dish to cover.

Ginger Pumpkin

Ingredients

500g/1lb Jap pumpkin   2 teaspoons oil
1 teaspoon fresh chopped ginger   salt, pepper
$^1/_2$ teaspoon nutmeg

Method

1. Cut pumpkin into $^1/_2$ cm/$^1/_5$ in slices. Place in a foil baking tray. Mix the ginger, nutmeg, oil, salt and pepper together and pour over the pumpkin. Place on the hotplate and cook for 10–15 minutes. Turn pieces over halfway through cooking.

   Note: Pumpkin may also be cooked directly on the oiled grill bars. Brush pumpkin slices with oil and sprinkle with salt. Place on the grill bars and cook 5 minutes on each side. Sprinkle with nutmeg and ginger before serving.

Whole Glazed Onions

Ingredients

24 or more small pickling onions   1$^1/_2$ cup red wine & garlic
2 teaspoons oil   marinade (page 90)
$^1/_2$ cup water

Method

1. Peel onions and cut a cross in the root end to prevent center from popping out. Place in a foil baking tray and add oil and water

2. Place on the barbecue when it is first lit. The onions can be heating as the barbecue heats.

3. When the onions commence to soften and the water evaporates, add the red wine and garlic marinade. Stir to coat onions well, and continue to cook until onions are well glazed and tender. Time will depend on heat of barbecue. It could take 30 minutes or more. Serve to accompany barbecued meats. Serves 8

Glazed Kumara

Ingredients

1kg/2¼lb Kumara (sweet potato) peeled and sliced
1 tablespoon water

1 cup red wine & garlic marinade (page 90)

Method

1. Grease the base of a foil baking tray. Arrange the sweet potato slices. Add the tablespoon of water. Brush the top of the sweet potato with the red wine marinade. Cover tray with foil, place on the hotplate and cook 10 minutes. Remove cover, turn slices over and brush with more marinade. Continue to cook uncovered until tender and well glazed.

Note: White sweet potato may also be used.

Jacket Potatoes

Ingredients

Cook over indirect heat in a covered barbecue.

1kg/2¼lb chat potatoes, washed
½ cup olive oil
3 teaspoons salt

1 cup sour cream
2 tablespoons Dijon mustard

Method

1. Toss potatoes with oil and salt to coat. Wrap each potato in a piece of foil. Place on the barbecue for 20–25 minutes, turn every 5 minutes. Split open and serve with sour cream mixed with the Dijon mustard.

Garlic Hot Cakes
with Sour Cream and Relish

Ingredients

1 cup self-raising flour
pinch salt
½ cup milk
1 egg

1 tspn crushed garlic
1 teaspoon parsley flakes
300g/10½oz carton sour cream
255g/9oz jar vegetable relish

Method

1. Sift flour and salt together into a bowl.

2. Beat together the milk, egg, garlic and parsley flakes, pour into the flour all at once and lightly stir until mixed in. Do not overmix.

3. Grease the hot hotplate of the barbecue. The best way to do this is to hold a wad of kitchen paper with tongs, dip the top of the wad in oil and rub over the hotplate.

4. Drop a tablespoon of the mixture from the tip end of the spoon onto the hotplate. When brown underneath and bubbles appear on the surface, turn with spatula to cook other side.

5. Lift into a cloth lined tray or basket as they cook, cover and serve warm. To serve, top with sour cream or cream cheese and a teaspoon of relish. Yield 24

Noodle and Vegetable Toss

Ingredients

455g/16oz Hokkein noodles
1 large carrot, coarsely grated
2 zucchini (courgette), grated
6 shallots, chopped into 2$\frac{1}{2}$cm/ in pieces

1 cup teriyaki marinade
(page 89)

Method

1. Rinse noodles in hot water and separate. Drain very well. Combine prepared vegetables. Place teriyaki marinade in a small saucepan to heat.

2. Heat the barbecue hotplate to medium-high and oil well. Pile on noodles, toss around a little and add vegetables. Lift and toss with tongs to mix through, then begin splashing on the heated marinade. When well mixed and heated through, remove to a hot serving plate. Serve immediately.

Pesto Potato Wedges

Ingredients

4 medium-sized potatoes
1 teaspoon crushed garlic
2 tablespoons basil pesto

1 tablespoon water
$\frac{1}{2}$ cup grated Parmesan cheese

Method

1. Peel and halve the potatoes, then cut each half into 4–6 wedges. Rinse well and drain then place in a large bowl. Mix garlic, basil pesto, olive oil and water together. Pour over potatoes and toss to coat well. Place in a large foil dish in a single layer if possible and pour over any basil oil mixture remaining in the bowl.

2. Cook over indirect heat in covered barbecue for 40 minutes, turning after 20 minutes. For flattop barbecue, cover with a sheet of foil and place foil tray on the hotplate. Cook 20 minutes then turn and cook 20 minutes more until tender.

3. When cooked, remove to a plate and sprinkle with Parmesan cheese.

Corn On the Cob

Ingredients

4 corns cobs
100g/3$\frac{1}{2}$oz butter
1 clove garlic, crushed

black pepper
shallots

Method

1. Spread corn with combined butter and garlic.

2. Preheat grill for 5 minutes on HIGH, cook for 4-5 minutes turning frequently.

3. Serve spinkled with shallots.

   Serves 4

Pesto Tomatoes

12 small even sized tomatoes
2 tablespoons basil pesto

2 tablespoons grated Romano
or Parmesan cheese

Method

1. Slice across top of tomato, leaving flap attached. Mix the basil and grated cheese together, lift tomato flap and spread onto the cut surface. Replace flap and spread a little on top. Stand in a foil tray and place tray on the barbecue. Cover with lid or hood and cook for 15 minutes. If flattop barbecue is used, cover tomatoes with foil.

Quick Ratatouille

Ingredients

2 medium-sized eggplants
(aubergine),
cut into 1cm/^{1}/$_2$in slices
4 zucchinis (courgettes), cut into
1cm/^{1}/$_2$in slices
1 large onion, cut in half & sliced

1 green capsicum (bell pepper),
seeded & sliced
300g/10^1/$_2$oz jar tomato salsa
1 teaspoon crushed garlic

Method

1. Prepare vegetables. Oil a large foil tray and spread base with some of the salsa. Layer in the vegetables, spreading salsa between each layer. Cover with more salsa. Place over indirect heat in kettle of covered barbecue and cook for 30 minutes. For flattop barbecue, cover tray with foil, stand on a cake-rake placed over the grill bars and cook for 30 minutes.

Polenta Toast

Ingredients

4 cups water
1 teaspoon salt
1 cup polenta
85g/3oz butter

^{1}/$_2$ cup grated Parmesan cheese
2 teaspoons chopped basil
^{1}/$_4$ cup olive oil

Method

1. Bring water and salt to the boil in a large saucepan. Add polenta and stir continuously until it begins to thicken. Reduce heat to low and simmer slowly for 20–30 minutes. Remove from heat and stir in the butter, Parmesan cheese and chopped basil.

2. Grease a 25 x 35cm/10 x 14in baking dish and pour in the polenta, spreading evenly to about 2^1/$_2$cm/1in thick. Chill in the refrigerator 1–2 hours.

3. Cut the chilled polenta into squares or rectangle shapes about 7cm/3in square. Remove from the dish, brush both sides with oil and place on heated grill bars. Cook about 5 minutes on each side. Serve hot to accompany barbecue meals.

gourmet
barbecue grill

This chapter is devoted to simple foods but with a gourmet touch, these may be cooked outdoors on the barbecue or indoors on electric barbecue grills.

All foods in this section are cooked on flat-top barbecues, charcoal, gas or electric. Electric barbecue grills or chargrills come in various sizes, from large hooded models to smaller chargrills units. Top-of-stove cooking is combined with barbecue cooking in this section.

Chicken Gado

455g/1lb chicken tenderloins
1 cup satay marinade (page 89)
1 ½ cups uncooked rice

200g/7oz green beans,
topped, tailed and halved
55g/2oz roasted unsalted peanuts

Method

1. Place tenderloins in a non-metal dish and stir in enough marinade to coat well. Cover and stand to marinate 30 minutes, or longer in refrigerator. Cook rice in boiling, salted water until tender, about 15 minutes. Drain well. Boil beans until tender but still crisp, drain. Mix rice, beans and half the roasted peanuts together. Keep hot.

2. Place a sheet of baking paper on top of hot grill bars and place the tenderloins on the paper. Cook for 2 minutes on each side on high heat, brushing with marinade during cooking. Heat extra marinade, about ½ cup, on side of barbecue.

3. Pile rice into centre of heated plates. Arrange 2 or 3 tenderloins over the rice, top with heated satay marinade and sprinkle with remaining cup-full of roasted peanuts.

Serves 5

68

Coriander Swordfish Steaks

Ingredients

115g/4oz unsalted butter

2 tablespoons finely chopped
coriander

1 tablespoon grated parmesan
cheese

4 swordfish steaks

1 tablespoon olive oil

4 zucchinis (courgettes), cut into
long slices

1 red capsicum (bell pepper),
quartered

Method

1. Cream the butter until soft and mix in the coriander and parmesan. Pile into butter pot and set aside.

2. Heat barbecue grill until hot and brush with oil. Brush fish steaks with oil, place on grill bars and cook 3–4 minutes each side according to thickness. Brush or spray vegetables with oil and place on grill, cook a few minutes on each side. Remove fish steaks and vegetables to heated plates. Top swordfish steak with a generous dollop of coriander butter mixture and serve immediately.

Serves 4

Garlic Lobster Tails
with Exotic Salad

Ingredients

6 green (raw) lobster tails
85g/3oz butter, softened
2 teaspoons crushed garlic
2 tablespoons honey and
lemon marinade (page 91)

Exotic Salad
1 avocado, cut into $^1/_2$ cm/$^1/_4$in dice
2 lebanese cucumbers, diced
$^1/_2$ small rockmelon, peeled & diced
$^1/_3$ cup honey and lemon marinade
(page 90)

Method

1. With kitchen scissors, cut each side of the soft shell on the underside of the lobster tails, and remove. Run a metal skewer through the length of each tail to keep them flat while cooking. Soften the butter and mix in the garlic, and honey and lemon marinade. Spread a coating on the lobster meat.

2. Prepare salad before commencing to cook lobster tails. Mix the diced avocado, cucumber, and rockmelon together. Pour the honey and lemon marinade over the salad. Refrigerate until needed.

3. Heat the barbecue to medium-high and oil the grill bars. Place lobster tails shell-side down and cook until shell turns red. Spread with more butter and turn meat-side down and cook for 5–8 minutes or meat turns white. Turn again and cook 2 minutes more shell-side down. Remove skewers and place on warm plates. Dot with any remaining butter mixture and serve immediately with exotic salad.

Serves 4-6

Sesame Barbecued Prawns

Ingredients

1kg/2$^1/_4$lb medium-large king prawns
55ml/2fl oz olive oil
55ml/2fl oz red wine
4 shallots, finely chopped
1 teaspoon grated lemon zest

$^1/_2$ teaspoon cracked black peppercorns
12 bamboo skewers
(soaked in water for 30 minutes)
115g/4oz Sesame Seeds

Method

1. Peel and de-vein prawns (leaving the shell tails intact)

2. Combine oil, wine, shallots, lemon zest and pepper. Mix well

3. Thread the prawns onto bamboo skewers (about 3 per skewer)

4. Place the skewers in a shallow dish and pour the marinade over. Allow to marinate in the refrigerator for a minimum of one hour.

5. Roll the prawns in the toasted sesame seeds, pressing them on well. Refrigerate for about 30 minutes. Place on the barbecue and brush with marinade whilst grilling.

Serves 6

Ginger Salmon Steaks
with Snowpeas (mangetout) and Potato

Ingredients

2 teaspoons chopped ginger
$\frac{1}{2}$ teaspoon chopped chilli
2 tablespoons oil
1 tablespoon lime juice
2 teaspoons grated lime zest

4 salmon cutlets
3 medium sized potatoes, parboiled in their jackets
200g/7oz snow peas (mangetout), blanched

Method

1. Mix the ginger, chilli, oil, lime juice and zest together. Pour half into a shallow dish or plate. Place salmon cutlets in dish and pour over the remaining marinade. Stand 20 minutes before cooking.

2. Heat the flat-top or electric barbecue grill to medium-high and oil the grill bars. Cook salmon cutlets 4–5 minutes each side, brushing with marinade as they cook. While cooking, place blanched snow peas in foil and reheat on the barbecue. Slice the potatoes into 1cm/$\frac{1}{2}$ in slices. Brush with oil and cook on the hotplate or grill bars a few minutes on each side. Serve immediately.

Serves 4

72

Honey and Chilli Prawns

Ingredients

455g/1 lb green king prawns   **soaked bamboo skewers**
**1 quality honey and chilli
marinade (page 89)**

Method

1. Shell the prawns, leaving on the tails and de-vein. Place in a glass dish and add enough honey & chilli marinade to coat well. Cover and marinate in refrigerator for 1 hour. Thread the prawns onto skewers, either through the side or through the length.

2. Heat the barbecue to medium-high. Place a sheet of baking paper over the grill bars and place the prawns on the paper. Cook for 4–5 minutes each side: they will turn pink when cooked. Brush with marinade while cooking. Transfer to a platter. Remove skewers and serve immediately.

Hot Herbed Beef Salad

Ingredients

2 boneless beef sirloins, 2^1/$_2$cm/1 in thick
^{1}/$_2$ teaspoon crushed garlic
1 teaspoon chopped chilli
2 teaspoons oil
salt, pepper
mixed salad greens for serving

Herb Dressing
2 teaspoons basil pesto
1 teaspoon chopped chilli
1 tablespoon chopped parsley
^{1}/$_2$ cup chopped shallots
^{1}/$_2$ cup olive oil
^{1}/$_4$ cup vinegar

Method

1. Place the steaks in a shallow dish. Mix together the garlic, chilli, oil, salt and pepper and pour over the steaks. Cover and stand 30 minutes.

2. Heat the barbecue grill bars to high and oil the bars. Sear meat 2 minutes on each side then turn down heat a little or move steaks to cooler part of barbecue and cook for 8 minutes on each side. Brush with marinade during cooking. Rest 5 minutes before slicing.

3. Slice meat thinly and arrange on platter lined with salad greens. Mix dressing ingredients together and pour over the beef. Serve immediately with Barbecue Toast (page 84)

Serves 6

Lamb Fillets with Salsa Pilaf

Ingredients

2 lamb fillets (about 750g/1²/₃ lb)
¹/₂ teaspoon crushed garlic
1 tablespoon lemon juice
2 teaspoons olive oil
salt & pepper

Salsa Pilaf
1¹/₂ cups uncooked rice
6 cups boiling water
55g/2oz pine nuts, toasted
300g/10¹/₂oz jar tomato salsa
2 tablespoons currants

Method

1. Trim the lamb fillets, removing the fine silver membrane. Place in a dish and add garlic, lemon juice, oil, salt and pepper. Cover and stand 30 minutes. Cook the rice in the boiling, salted water, about 15 minutes, until rice is tender. Drain well and keep hot. Heat a small saucepan, add pine nuts and shake over heat until they colour. Add the salsa and currants and heat through.

2. Heat the barbecue grill plate and oil lightly. Set at medium-high. Place lamb on grill and cook 6-8 minutes, turning to cook on all sides. Cook longer for well done. Rest 5 minutes before slicing in 1cm/¹/₂ in slices.

3. To Serve: Using a cup or mould, form a mound of rice on the plate. Pour salsa over the rice and arrange lamb slices at base of rice mould.

Serves 4-5

Pork Fillets
with Garlic and Coriander Mash

Ingredients

1 pork fillet (about 455g/1lb)

1 tablespoon chopped coriander

Coriander Mash

400g/14oz potatoes peeled and cut

200g/7oz sweet potato (kumara), peeled and cut

boiling, salted water

1 teaspoon butter

$^1/_2$ cup milk

1$^1/_2$ teaspoons crushed garlic

2 tablespoons chopped coriander

Method

1. Remove the white connective tissue from the pork, then rub all over with coriander paste. Cover and stand 30 minutes at room temperature. Meanwhile, prepare the mash. Boil the potatoes and sweet potato until tender. Drain and return to the hot saucepan. Mash with a potato masher, add butter, milk, garlic and coriander. Whip well until smooth. Cover and keep hot.

2. Heat the barbecue grill bars to medium-high. Place pork fillet on grill and turn to sear on all sides. Lower heat and continue to cook for about 12–15 minutes until done to taste. Rest the fillet for 5 minutes wrapped in foil then cut into thick diagonal slices. Mound garlic and coriander mash on a plate and arrange slices of pork. Serve immediately.

Serves 3-4

Tandoori Chicken with Yoghurt Sauce

Ingredients

4 chicken breast fillets
2 tablespoons tandoori paste
(page 89)
Yoghurt Sauce
455g/1 lb natural yoghurt
2 lebanese cucumbers, diced

2 tablespoons tandoori paste
3–4 zucchinis (courgettes), sliced
boiled rice for serving
1 cup tomato & chilli pickle
for serving

Method

1. Rub the chicken fillets with the tandoori paste. Drizzle with a little extra paste, then cover and marinate for at least 30 minutes before cooking.

2. Mix the yoghurt, diced cucumber and remaining tandoori paste together. Cover and refrigerate until serving.

3. Heat the barbecue to medium-high and oil the grill bars. Place a piece of baking paper over the grill bars. Set the chicken and cook for 3–4 minutes each side. Place zucchini (courgette) slices onto well-oiled grill bars and cook both sides until tender but still crisp.

4. Slice the chicken on the diagonal. Place zucchini (courgette) slices on the plate, arrange on the chicken slices and mask with yoghurt sauce. Serve with hot, boiled rice and a spoonful of tomato chilli pickle.

Serves 4-5

Veal and Eggplant(aubergine) Stack with Salsa

Ingredients

4 veal steaks (scallopini)
1 teaspoon crushed garlic
1 tablespoon lemon juice
salt, pepper
1 large eggplant (aubergine), cut

into 4 slices lengthwise
300g/10^1/₂oz jar tomato salsa
4 slices Gruyere cheese
2 shallots, finely chopped

Method

1. Place the veal in a glass dish. Mix garlic, lemon juice, salt and pepper together and pour over the veal. Stand for 30 minutes before cooking.

2. Heat the barbecue grill until hot. Place salsa in a small saucepan and heat on side of the barbecue. Brush the eggplant (aubergine) on both sides with olive oil or spray with olive oil spray. Place on grill bars or hotplate and cook for 4 minutes on one side. Turn and cook second side. Place the veal scallopini onto the hot, oiled grill bars and cook 1 minute each side then lift and place each scallopini on top of a slice of eggplant (aubergine). Spread a spoonful of heated salsa over the veal and top with a slice of cheese. Swirl a little salsa over surface of cheese. Sprinkle with a few shallots and cover with lid or hood to complete cooking of eggplant (aubergine) and to melt the cheese slightly. Serve immediately with extra salsa.

Serves 4

Warm Thai Chicken Salad

Ingredients

3 chicken breasts

2 teaspoons Thai flavour base

I teaspoon oil

I red capsicum (bell pepper), seeded and cut into strips

I green capsicum (pepper). seeded
and cut into strips

I eggplant (aubergine), cut into slices

I spanish onion, cut into rings

$^1/_2$ cos lettuce, shredded

Dressing

$^1/_2$ cup olive oil

$^1/_4$ cup malt vinegar

I teaspoon Thai flavour base

Method

1. Flatten chicken breasts slightly to even thickness. Mix Thai flavour base and oil together and rub well into the chicken. Cover and stand 20 minutes before cooking.

2. Heat the barbecue to medium-high and oil hotplate and grill bars, place chicken on grill and cook 4 minutes each side. Place vegetables on the hotplate, drizzle with a little oil and cook for 5–8 minutes tossing and turning to cook through. Pile lettuce onto individual plates and place barbecued vegetables in the centre. Cut the chicken into thin diagonal slices and arrange over and around vegetables.

3. Mix dressing ingredients together and pour over chicken and warm salad. Serve with crusty bread.

Serves 3

interesting
additions

Interesting additions to barbecue food: fruit accompaniments, salad dressing, toasts, breads and others lift the interest and the enjoyment of barbecued foods.

Barbecue Toasts

Ingredients

Bread
Plain Facaccia
Turkish Bread
Mini Dampers
Bread Rolls
Firm Bread Loaf, sliced

Butters
butter or margarine
tandoori paste (page 89)
thai flavour base
pesto

Method

1. Mix one part butter or margarine with a part flavouring to taste. Lightly spread both sides of sliced bread or rolls with flavoured butter of your choice. Place on heated hot plate and cook until golden on both sides.

82

Corn Relish Muffins

Ingredients

1 cup self raising-flour
¹/₃ cup milk
1 ¹/₂ tablespoons melted butter

1 egg
¹/₂ cup corn relish

Method

1. Sift the flour into a bowl and make a well in the centre. Mix together the milk, melted butter, egg and corn relish. Pour mixture into the well of flour and quickly mix with a round-bladed knife into a soft dough. Do not overmix. Drop dough into 6 greased muffin pans. Place over indirect heat on barbecue or elevate on a wire cake-rack on grill bars over direct heat. Cover with lid or hood and cook for 20–25 minutes. If a browned top is desired, turn muffins over when cooked to ensure browning. Serve hot with butter.

Yields 6

Garlic and Herbed Breads

1 french bread stick (baguette)
55g/2 oz garlic or other flavoured
butter (see below)

Method

1. Cut the bread almost through at $^1/_2$ cm intervals. Lightly spread each cut surface with your choice of butter. Wrap in foil and place on the barbecue (to the side of other foods cooking). Cook for 20 minutes, turning frequently.

Capsicum (Bell Pepper) Butter –

Mix 2 tablespoons chopped roasted capsicum (bell pepper) into 55g/2oz soft butter.

Coriander Butter –

Mix 2 tablespoons of chopped coriander and $^1/_2$ teaspoon ground cumin into 55g/2oz softened butter.

Curried Butter –

Mix 2 teaspoons tandoori paste (page 89) and 2 teaspoons lemon juice into 55g/2oz softened butter.

Garlic Butter –

Soften 60g/2oz butter and mix in 2 teaspoons crushed garlic.

Lemongrass Butter –

Mix 2 teaspoons of lemongrass paste or 2 teaspoons grated lemon zest into 55g/2oz softened butter.

Tip: Flavoured butters may be formed into a roll, wrapped in plastic wrap and refrigerated, then cut into slices to place on top of barbecued steaks.

Olive Butter –

Stone and chop 10 black olives, then mix with 100g/3oz butter. Add 1 teaspoon freshly crushed garlic and mix well. Serve with lamb, eggplant (aubergine), duck or vegetable patties.

Pesto Butter –

Mix 2 teaspoons pesto and 2 tablespoons grated Parmesan cheese into 55g/2oz softened butter.

Savoury Anchovy Butter

Place 200g/7oz butter, 4 anchovy fillets, 2 spring chopped onions, 1 teaspoon freshly crushed garlic and one tablespoon of garted lemon zest in a food processor and process for about 30 seconds, until a smooth paste. Put into small serving pots and refrigerate until ready to use.

Glazed Bananas

Ingredients

4 bananas
¹/₂ cup honey & chilli
marinade (page 89)

Method

1. Peel bananas and slit in half lenthwise or cut into 5cm/2in pieces. Place on a sheet of baking paper, on the hot grill bars. Brush with marinade as they cook and turn occasionally. Cook until well glazed. Serve hot to accompany barbecued lamb or pork.

Melon Medley Salsa

Ingredients

¹/₂ rock melon   **¹/₂ cup red wine and**
¹/₂ honeydew melon   **garlic marinade (page 90)**

Method

1. Peel the melons and remove seeds, cut into large cubes. Pour the marinade into a foil dish and place on the heated hotplate. When it begins to bubble, add the melon cubes. Cook a few minutes, turn the cubes and baste with the marinade to glaze. Remove and serve with barbecued meats and chicken.

Peppered Pineapple

Ingredients

I small ripe, pineapple
I teaspoon chopped chilli

I tablespoon brown sugar
I tablespoon melted butter

Method

1. Combine the chopped chilli, brown sugar and melted butter together.

2. Peel the pineapple. Cut into rings and remove the core. Place on heated and oiled grill bars. Cook I minute on each side then brush with chilli mixture and cook 2 minutes each side. Serve with barbecued pork sausages, pork chops, steaks or chicken.

Stuffed Apples

Ingredients

6 small, red crisp apples
2$\frac{1}{2}$ cups fresh white breadcrumbs
I small onion, very finely chopped

salt, pepper
2 tablespoons honey & chilli marinade (page 89)
I tablespoon sultanas

Method

1. Remove the core from the apples with a small, pointed knife. Cut out more apple flesh to widen the hole. Chop the flesh finely and add to the breadcrumbs. Mix in remaining ingredients. Pack the stuffing into the apples. Place apples in a foil tray and brush over with honey & chilli marinade.

2. Place on barbecue using indirect heat or elevate on wire rack over direct heat. Cover with lid or hood and cook for 30 minutes. Serve as an accompaniment to roast pork or roast turkey.

Stuffed Mushrooms

Ingredients

12 medium mushrooms
$\frac{1}{2}$ red capsicum (bell pepper), chopped finely
I cup fresh breadcrumbs
I teaspoon crushed garlic

I tablespoon parsley, chopped
I spring onion, chopped
$\frac{1}{2}$ cup grated Parmesan cheese
2 tablespoons melted butter

Method

1. Remove stalks from mushrooms. Combine stuffing ingredients and spoon generously into each mushroom. Sprinkle with a little extra Parmesan cheese.

2. Place on barbecue, cover and grill for 5 minutes, or until tender.

   Makes 12

Sauces

Chilli-Strawberry Sauce –

Ingredients

$1/2$ medium onion, chopped
1 teaspoon freshly crushed garlic
1 tablespoon olive oil
$1/2$ cup tomato sauce (ketchup)
$1/2$ cup strawberry jam

$1/4$ cup beer
2 hot chillis, seeded and
finely chopped
1 tablespoon barbecue sauce
1 teaspoon chilli flakes

Method

1. In a small saucepan cook onion and garlic until soft. Stir in all other ingredients and bring to high simmer, do not boil/reduce heat. Cook uncovered for about 10 minutes stirring occasionally, until mixture thickens. Keep handy to the barbecue to brush on meat whilst cooking.

Curry Sauce –

Ingredients

$1^1/2$ tablespoons butter
1 tablespoon flour
$1/2$ teaspoon curry powder
1 cup milk

salt
freshly ground black pepper,
to taste
1 tablespoon mango chutney

Method

1. Melt butter in a saucepan, add flour and curry powder, stir until smooth. Remove from heat. Gradually add milk, stirring continously. Return to heat and return to heat until sauce boils and thickens. Cook for an extra minute.

Peanut Sauce –

Ingredients

2 tblspns crunchy peanut butter
1 onion finely chopped
$1/4$ teaspoon chilli flakes

2 tablespoons lemon juice
$1/4$ cup water

Method

1. Combine all ingredients in a saucepan and simmer gently until thickened. Handy to keep warm on the side of the barbecue.

Sweet & Sour Sauce –

Ingredients

$1/3$ cup vinegar
1 tblspn soy sauce
$4^1/2$ tablespoons sugar
1 tablespoon tomato sauce

2 tblspns Worchestershire sauce
$1/2$ teaspoon salt
1 teaspoon freshly chopped ginger

Method

1. Combine all ingredients together and stir over low heat until sauce thickens. If a thicker sauce is desired add a $1/2$ teaspoon blended cornflour.

Marinades

We recommend that you try the MasterFoods range of marinades, you will find them easy to use and they give fantastic results. If however you wish to make your own, hereunder are a couple of interesting ones to try.

Honey & Chilli Marinade

Ingredients

1/4 cup red wine
1/2 cup honey
1/4 teaspoon ground chilli

1 teaspoon mustard powder
Mix well together

Method: Mix all ingredients together

Satay Marinade

Ingredients

1/2 cup peanut butter
1/2 teaspoon chilli powder
1/2 teaspoon ground ginger

2 tablespoon lemon juice
1 tablespoon brown sugar
1/2 cup coconut milk

Method: Place all ingredients in a pan, heat and stir to combine. Allow to cool.

Teriyaki Marinade

Ingredients

1/2 cup soy sauce
2 tablespoons brown sugar
1/2 teaspoon ground ginger

2 tablespoon wine vinegar
1 clove garlic, crushed
2 tablespoons tomato sauce

Method: Mix all ingredients together.

Herbed Wine Marinade

Ingredients

1/2 cup red wine
2 tsp mixed dried herbs
1 tablespoon red wine vinegar

2 tablespoon olive oil
1 clove garlic, crushed
1 tsp hot English mustard

Method: Place all ingredients in a pan, heat and stir to combine. Allow to cool.

Tandoori Paste

Ingredients

2 cloves garlic, peeled
2 1/2cm/1 in peeled fresh ginger chopped
1 teaspoon salt
2 teaspoons coriander seeds
2 tablespoons lemon juice

2 tablespoons vinegar
1 teaspoon cumin seeds
1/2 teaspoon chilli powder
1 teaspoon tumeric
1/2 cup plain yoghurt

Method: Blend all ingredients except the yoghurt in an electric blender to a smooth paste. Stir into the yoghurt

Marinades

Soy and Honey Marinade

Ingredients

¼ cup soy sauce

2 tablespoons honey

I tablespoon sherry

2 cloves garlic, crushed

I teaspoon grated fresh ginger

Red Wine & Garlic Marinade

Ingredients

½ cup red wine

¼ cup brown sugar

2 cloves garlic, crushed

salt, pepper

Method: Place all ingredients in a pan, heat and stir to combine. Allow to cool.

Ginger-Rum Marinade –

Ingredients

½ cup unsweeted pineapple

⅓ cup light rum

¼ cup soy sauce

I tablespoon chopped ginger

2 teaspoons crushed garlic

I tablespoon brown sugar

¼ teaspoon chilli powder

Lime-Garlic Marinade –

Ingredients

½ cup chicken stock

⅓ cup lime juice

2 tablespoons olive oil

I tablespoon brown sugar

3 teaspoons crushed garlic

¼ teaspoon chilli powder

¼ teaspoon mint flakes

or ½ teaspoon chopped fresh mint

Moroccan Lamb Marinade –

Ingredients

2 tablespoons parsley flakes

I tablespoon lemon juice

¼ teaspoon ground cummin

¼ teaspoon black pepper

¼ teaspoon cayenne pepper

¼ teaspoon ground ginger

¼ teaspoon ground coriander seeds

Method: Combine all ingredients in a bowl, stir to a paste. Spread marinade over both sides of lamb and stand for I hour at room temperature, or up to 4 hours in refrigerator.

Honey and Lemon Marinade –

Ingredients

½ cup olive oil

2 tablespoons lemon juice

I tablespoon honey

I tablespoon freshly crushed garlic

2 bay leaves, crushed

Method: Mix all ingredients together

Marinades

Marinating foods has two purposes. Firstly to impart delightful flavours and secondly, but equally important, to tenderise the meats. The following points will guide you.

- Do not use a metal container to marinate food, the acid base reacts with the metal and can taint the flavour. Use glass, ceramic, stainless steel or firm plastic. Do not use ice cream containers.

- Do not marinate foods for longer than 20–30 minutes at room temperature, as microbial activity will commence ofter this. Longer marinating must be place in the refrigerator.

- Tougher cuts of meat, eg. forequarter cuts, round and topside cuts, need long marinating to tenderise them. Do overnight marinating in the refrigerator.

- The sugar or honey content in some marinades causes the food to char quickly. To avoid this, elevate the food on a wire rack about 1cm/1/2 in above the grill bars. Place the wire rack lengthwise so the feet can go down a little way reducing the distance between bars and rock, or, if a high temperature is used, place it widthwise so the feet will stand on the bars and the distance will be 2$\frac{1}{2}$cm/1 in above the bars.

- Another method is to place a sheet of baking paper on the grill bars and cook the food on the paper. The marks of the bars will still transfer onto the food, giving the chargilled appearance. Cut a few slashes between the bars to aid air circulation and obtain the smoky barbecue taste. For gas barbecues, heat well before covering bars with baking paper and turn down the flame when baking paper is placed on to avoid burning the paper. Fuel barbecues may scorch the paper if left on too long, if this happens, replace with fresh paper to complete cooking. The result is worth the effort. Electric barbecue grills have no problem with this method.

- To glaze meats with marinade, cook the meat until it browns and firms a little then brush with marinade every few minutes, turning meat to glaze all sides.

- Remaining marinades, which had contact with the meat during the marinatng process, can be used for brushing the meat while cooking, but MUST be discarded when cooking is completed. Do not use as a sauce, use fresh marinade from the bottle.

Note: There are many prepared marinades available now in all supermarkets which can be used in place of the marinade recipes given. Look for the flavour to suit your taste and the food it is to be used with.

Glossary

acidulated water: water with added acid, such as lemon juice or vinegar, which prevents discolouration of ingredients, particularly fruit or vegetables; the proportion of acid to water is 1 teaspoon per 300mL

al dente: Italian cooking term for ingredients that are cooked until tender but still firm to the bite; usually applied to pasta

americaine: method of serving seafood—usually lobster and monkfish—in a sauce flavoured with olive oil, aromatic herbs, tomatoes, white wine, fish stock, brandy and tarragon

an glaise: cooking style for simple cooked dishes such as boiled vegetables; assiette an glaise is a plate of cold cooked meats

antipasto: Italian for 'before the meal'; it denotes an assortment of cold meats,vegetables and cheeses, often marinated, served as an hors d'œuvre; a typical antipasto might include salami, prosciutto, marinated artichoke hearts, anchovy fillets, olives, tuna fish and Provolone cheese

au gratin: food sprinkled with breadcrumbs, often covered with cheese sauce and browned until a crisp coating forms

balsamic vinegar: a mild, extremely fragrant wine-based vinegar made in northern Italy; traditionally, the vinegar is aged for at least seven years in a series of casks made of various woods

baste: to moisten food while it is cooking by spooning or brushing on liquid or fat

baine marie: a saucepan standing in a large pan which is filled with boiling water to keep liquids at simmering point; a double boiler will do the same job

beat: to stir thoroughly and vigorously

beurre manie: equal quantities of butter and flour kneaded together and added a little at a time to thicken a stew or casserole

bird: see paupiette

blanc: a cooking liquid made by adding flour and lemon juice to water in order to keep certain vegetables from discolouring as they cook

blanch: to plunge into boiling water and then (in some cases) into coldwater; fruits and nuts are blanched to remove skin easily

blanquette: a white stew of lamb, veal or chicken, bound with egg yolks and cream, and accompanied by onion and mushrooms

blend: to mix thoroughly

bonne femme: dishes cooked in the traditional French 'housewife' style; chicken and pork bonne femme are garnished with bacon, potatoes and baby onion; fish bonne femme with mushrooms in a white wine sauce

bouquet garni: a bunch of herbs, usually consisting of sprigs of parsley, thyme, marjoram, rosemary, a bayleaf, peppercorns and cloves, tied in muslin and used to flavour stews and casseroles

braise: to cook whole or large pieces of poultry, game, fish, meat or vegetables in a small amount of wine, stock or other liquid in a closed pot; often the main ingredient is first browned in fat and then cooked in a low oven or very slowly on top of the stove; braising suits tough meats and older birds, and produces a mellow, rich sauce

broil: the American term for grilling food

brown: to cook in a small amount of fat until brown

bulgur: a type of cracked wheat in which the kernels are steamed and dried before being cracked

buttered: to spread with softened or melted butter

butterfly: to slit a piece of food in half horizontally, cutting it almost through so that when opened it resembles butterfly wings; chops, large prawns and thick fish fillets are often butterflied so that they cook more quickly

buttermilk: a tangy, low-fat cultured milk product the slight acidity of which makes it an ideal marinade base for poultry

calzone: a semicircular pocket of pizza dough, stuffed with meat or vegetables, sealed and baked

caramelise: to melt sugar until it is a golden brown syrup

champignons: small mushrooms, usually canned

chasseur: (hunter) a French cooking style in which meat and chicken dishes are cooked with mushrooms, shallots, white wine, and often tomato

clarify: to melt butter and drain the oil off the sediment

coat: to cover with a thin layer of flour, sugar, nuts, crumbs, poppy or sesame seeds, cinnamon sugar or a few of the ground spices

concasser: to chop coarsely, usually tomatoes

confit: from the French verb confire, meaning to preserve; refers to food that is made into a preserve by cooking very slowly and thoroughly until tender; in the case of meat (such as duck or goose) it is cooked in its own fat, and covered with it,

so that it does not come into contact with the air; vegetables such as onions are good in confit

consommé: a clear soup usually made from beef

coulis: a thin purée, usually of fresh or cooked fruit or vegetables, which is soft enough to pour (couler means to run); a coulis may be rough-textured or very smooth

court bouillon: the liquid in which fish, poultry or meat is cooked; it usually consists of water with bayleaf, onion, carrots and salt (and freshly ground black pepper to taste); other additives can include wine, vinegar, stock, garlic or spring onions (scallions)

couscous: cereal processed from semolina into pellets, traditionally steamed and served with meat and vegetables in the classic North African stew of the same name

cruciferous vegetables:
certain members of the mustard, cabbage and turnip families with cross-shaped flowers and strong aromas and flavours

cream: to make soft, smooth and creamy by rubbing with back of spoon or by beating with mixer; usually applied to fat and sugar

croûtons: small toasted or fried cubes of bread

crudites: raw vegetables, whether cutin slices or sticks, to nibble plain or with a dipping sauce, or shredded and tossed as salad with a simple dressing

cube: to cut into small pieces with 6 equal sides

curdle: to cause milk or sauce to separate into solid and liquid (for example, overcooked egg mixtures)

daikon radish: (also called mooli): a long white Japanese radish

dark sesame oil: (also called Oriental sesame oil): dark polyunsaturated oil with a low burning point, used for seasoning; (do not replace with lighter sesame oil)

deglaze: to dissolve congealed cooking juices or glaze on the bottom of a pan by adding a liquid, then scraping and stirring vigorously whilst bringing the liquid to the boil; juices may be used to make gravy or to add to sauce

degrease: to skim grease from the surface of liquid; if possible the liquid should be chilled so the fat solidifies; if not, skim off most of the fat with a large metal spoon, then trail strips of paper towel on the surface of the liquid to remove any remaining globules

devilled: a dish or sauce that is highly seasoned with a hot ingredient such as mustard, Worcestershire sauce or cayenne pepper

dice: to cut into small cubes

dietary-fibre: a plant-cell material that is undigested or only partially digested in the human body, but which promotes healthy digestion of other food matter

dissolve: mix a dry ingredient with liquid until absorbed

dredge: to coat with a dry ingredient, such as flour or sugar

drizzle: to pour in a fine thread-like stream over a surface

dust: to sprinkle or coat lightly with flour or icing sugar

Dutch oven: a heavy casserole with a lid, usually made from cast iron or pottery

emulsion: a mixture of two liquids that are not mutually soluble—for example, oil and water

entrée: in Europe, the 'entry' or hors d'œuvre; in North America entrée means the main course

fillet: special cut of beef, lamb, pork or veal; breast of poultry and game; fish cut off the bone lengthways

flake: to break into small pieces with a fork

flame: to ignite warmed alcohol over food

fold-in: a gentle, careful combining of a light or delicate mixture with a heavier mixture using a metal spoon

fricassee: a dish in which poultry, fish or vegetables are bound together with a white or veloute sauce; in Britain and the United States, the name applies to an old-fashioned dish of chicken in a creamy sauce

galette: sweet or savoury mixture shaped as a flat round

garnish: to decorate food, usually with something edible

gastrique:
caramelised sugar deglazed with vinegar and used in fruit-flavoured savoury sauces, in such dishes as duck with orange

glaze: a thin coating of beaten egg, syrup or aspic which is brushed over pastry, fruits or cooked meats

gluten: a protein in flour that is developed when dough is kneaded, making it elastic

gratin: a dish cooked in the oven or under the grill so that it develops a brown crust; bread crumbs or cheese may be sprinkled on top first; shallow gratin dishes ensure a maximum area of crust

grease: to rub or brush lightly with oil or fat

joint: to cut poultry, game or small animals into serving pieces by dividing at the joint

julienne: to cut food into match-like strips

knead: to work dough using the heel of the hand with a pressing motion, while stretching and folding the dough

line: to cover the inside of a container with paper, to protect or aid in removing mixture

infuse: to immerse herbs, spices or other flavourings in hot liquid to flavour it; infusion takes from 2–5 minutes depending on the flavouring; the liquid should be very hot but not boiling

jardiniere: a garnish of garden vegetables, typically carrots, pickling onions, French beans and turnips

lights: lungs of an animal, used in various meat preparations such as pâtès and faggots

macerate: to soak food in liquid to soften

marinade: a seasoned liquid, usually an oil and acid mixture, in which meats or other foods are soaked to soften and give more flavour

marinara:
Italian 'sailor's style' cooking that does not apply to any particular combination of ingredients; marinara tomato sauce for pasta is most familiar

marinate: to let food stand in a marinade to season and tenderise

mask: to cover cooked food with sauce

melt: to heat until liquified

mince: to grind into very small pieces

mix: to combine ingredients by stirring

monounsaturated fats: one of three types of fats found in foods; are believed not to raise the level of cholesterol in the blood

niçoise: a garnish of tomatoes, garlic and black olives; a salad with anchovy, tuna and French beans is typical

non-reactive pan: a cooking pan the surface of which does not chemically react with food; materials used include stainless steel, enamel, glass and some alloys

noisette: small 'nut' of lamb cut from boned loin or rack that is rolled, tied and cut in neat slices; noisette also means flavoured with hazel nuts, or butter cooked to a nut brown colour

normande: a cooking style for fish, with a garnish of shrimp, mussels and mushrooms in a white wine cream sauce; for poultry and meat, a sauce with cream, Calvados and apple

olive oil: various grades of oil extract from olives; extra virgin olive oil has a full, fruity flavour and the lowest acidity; virgin olive oil is slightly higher in acidity and lighter in flavour; pure olive oil is a processed blend of olive oils and has the highest acidity and lightest taste

panade: a mixture for binding stuffings and dumplings, notably quenelles, often of choux pastry or simply bread crumbs; a panade may also be made of fran gipane, puréed potatoes or rice

papillote: to cook food in oiled or buttered greasepoof paper or aluminium foil; also a decorative frill to cover bone ends of chops and poultry drumsticks

parboil: to boil or simmer until part-cooked (that is, cooked further than when blanching)

pare: to cut away outside covering

pâtè: a paste of meat or seafood used as a spread for toast or crackers

paupiette: a thin slice of meat, poultry or fish spread with a savoury stuffing and rolled; in the United States this is also called 'bird' and in Britain an 'olive'

peel: to strip away outside covering

plump: to soak in liquid or moisten thoroughly until full and round

poach: to simmer gently in enough hot liquid to cover, using care to retain shape of food

polyunsaturated fat: one of the three types of fats found in food; these exist in large quantities in such vegetable oils as safflower, sunflower, corn and soyabean; these fats lower the level of cholesterol in the blood

purée: a smooth paste, usually of vegetables or fruits, made by putting foods through a sieve, food mill or liquefying in a blender or food processor

ragout: traditionally a well-seasoned, rich stew containing meat, vegetables and wine; nowadays, a term applied to any stewed mixture

ramekins:
small oval or round individual baking dishes

reconstitute: to put moisture back into dehydrated foods by soaking in liquid

reduce: to cook over a very high heat, uncovered, until the liquid is reduced by evaporation

refresh: to cool hot food quickly, either under running water or by plunging it into iced water, to stop it cooking; particularly for vegetables and occasionally for shellfish

rice vinegar: mild, fragrant vinegar that is less sweet than cider vinegar and not as harsh as distilled malt vinegar; Japanese rice vinegar is milder than the Chinese variety

roulade: a piece of meat, usually pork or veal, that is spread with stuffing, rolled and often braised or poached; a roulade may also be a sweet or savoury mixture that is baked in a Swiss roll tin or paper case, filled with a contrasting filling, and rolled

rubbing-in: a method of incorporating fat into flour, by use of fingertips only; also incorporates air into mixture

safflower oil:
the vegetable oil that contains the highest proportion of polyunsaturated fats

salsa: a juice derived from the main ingredient being cooked or a sauce added to a dish to enhance its flavour; in Italy the term is often used for pasta sauces; in Mexico the name usually applies to uncooked sauces served as an accompaniment, especially to corn chips

saturated fats: one of the three types of fats found in foods; these exist in large quantities in animal products, coconut and palm oils; they raise the level of cholesterol in the blood; as high cholesterol levels may cause heart disease, saturated fat consumption is recommended to be less than 15 per cent of kilojoules provided by the daily diet

sauté: to cook or brown in small amount of hot fat

score: to mark food with cuts, notches of lines to prevent curling or to make food more attractive

scald: to bring just to boiling point, usually for milk; also to rinse with boiling water

sear: to brown surface quickly over high heat in hot dish

seasoned flour: flour with salt and pepper added

self raising flour: sometimes called "pancake flour" or "self rising flour". Main difference between plain white flour and self raising flour is self raising flour contains 360mg/oz of sodium per serve and less potassium of 40mg/oz

sift: to shake a dry, powdered substance through a sieve or sifter to remove any lumps and give lightness

simmer: to cook food gently in liquid that bubbles steadily just below boiling point so that the food cooks in even heat without breaking up

singe: to quickly flame poultry to remove all traces of feathers after plucking

skim: to remove a surface layer (often of impurities and scum) from a liquid with a metal spoon or small ladle

slivered: sliced in long, thin pieces; usually refers to nuts, especially almonds

soften: re gelatine—sprinkle over cold water and allow to gel (soften) then dissolve and liquefy

souse: to cover food, particularly fish, in wine vinegar and spices and cook slowly; the food is cooled in the same liquid; sousing gives food a pickled flavour

steep: to soak in warm or cold liquid in order to soften food and draw out strong flavours or impurities

stir-fry: to cook thin slices of meat and vegetable over a high heat in a small amount of oil, stirring constantly to cook evenly in a short time; traditionally cooked in a wok, however a heavy-based frying pan may be used

stock: a liquid containing flavours, extracts and nutrients of bones, meat, fish or vegetables

stud: to adorn with; for example, baked ham studded with whole cloves

sugo: an Italian sauce made from the liquid or juice extracted from fruit or meat during cooking

sweat: to cook sliced or chopped food, usually vegetables, in a little fat and no liquid over very low heat; GLAD-Foil is pressed on top so that the food steams in its own juices, usually before being added to other dishes

timbale: a creamy mixture of vegetables or meat baked in a mould; French for 'kettle-drum'; also denotes a drum-shaped baking dish

thicken: to make a thin, smooth paste by mixing together arrowroot, cornflour or flour with an equal amount of cold water; stir into hot liquid, cook, stirring until thickened

toss: to gently mix ingredients with two forks or fork and spoon

total fat: the individual daily intake of all three fats previously described in this glossary; nutritionists recommend that fats provide no more than 35 per cent of the energy in the diet

vine leaves: tender, lightly flavoured leaves of the grapevine, used in ethnic cuisine as wrappers for savoury mixtures; as the leaves are usually packed in brine, they should be well rinsed before use

whip: to beat rapidly, incorporate air and produce expansion

zest: thin outer layer of citrus fruits containing the aromatic citrus oil; it is usually thinly pared with a vegetable peeler, or grated with a zester or grater to separate it from the bitter white pith underneath

Weights and Measures

Cooking is not an exact science: one does not require finely calibrated scales, pipettes and scientific equipment to cook, yet the conversion to metric measures in some countries and its interpretations must have intimidated many a good cook.

Weights are given in the recipes only for ingredients such as meats, fish, poultry and some vegetables, necessary for marketing anyway, though a few grams or ounces one way or another will not affect the success of your dish.

Though recipes have been tested using the Australian Standard 250mL cup, 20mL tablespoon and 5mL teaspoon, they will work just as well with the US and Canadian 8 fluid ounce cup, or the UK 300mL cup. We have used graduated cup measures in preference to tablespoon measures so that proportions are always the same. Where tablespoon measures have been given, these are not crucial measures, so using the smaller tablespoon of the US or UK will not affect the recipe's success. At least we all agree on the teaspoon size.

For breads, cakes, pastries, etc. the only area which might cause concern is where eggs are used, as proportions will then vary. If working with a 250mL or 300mL cup, use large eggs (55g or 2oz), adding a little more liquid to the recipe for 300ml cup measures if it seems necessary. Use the medium sized eggs (55g or 2oz) with 8fl oz cup measure. A graduated set of measuring cups and spoons is recommended, the cups in particular for measuring dry ingredients. Remember to level such ingredients.

English and American Measures

English

All measurements are similar to Australian with two exceptions: the English cup measures 10 fluid ounces (300mL), whereas the Australian cup measure 8 fluid ounces (250mL). The English tablespoon (the Australian dessertspoon) measures 14.8mL against the Australian tablespoon of 20mL.

American

The American reputed pint is 16 fl oz, a quart is equal to 32 fl oz and the American gallon, 128 fl oz. The Imperial measurement is 20 fl oz to the pint, 40 fl oz a quart and 160 fl oz one gallon. The American tablespoon is equal to 14.8mL, the teaspoon is 5mL. The cup measure is 8 fluid ounces (250mL), the same as Australia.

Dry Measures

All the measures are level, so when you have filled a cup or spoon, level it off with the edge of a knife.

The scale below is the "cook's equivalent", it is not an exact conversion of metric to imperial measurement.

The exact metric equivalent is 2.2046lb = 1kg

or 1lb = 0.45359kg

METRIC		IMPERIAL	
g = grams		oz = ounces	
kg = kilograms		lb = pound	
15g		1/2oz	
20g		2/3oz	
30g		1oz	
55g		2oz	
85g		3oz	
115g		4oz	1/4lb
125g		41/2oz	
145g		5oz	
170g		6oz	
225g		8oz	1/2lb
255g		9oz	
285g		10oz	
315g		11oz	
340g		12oz	3/4lb
370g		13oz	
400g		14oz	
425g		15oz	
455g		16oz	
500g	1kg	171/2oz	2.2lb
11/2kg		31/3lb	

Oven Temperatures

The Celsius temperatures given here are not exact; they have been rounded off and are given as a guide only. Follow the manufacturer's temperature guide, relating it to oven description given in the recipe. Remember gas ovens are hottest at the top, electric ovens at the bottom and convection-fan forced ovens are usually even throughout. We included Regulo numbers for gas cookers which may assist. To convert °C to °F multiply °C by 9 and divide by 5 then add 32.

	C°	F°	REGULO
Very slow	120	250	1
Slow	150	300	2
Moderately slow	150	325	3
Moderate	180	350	4
Moderately hot	190-200	370-400	5-6
Hot	210-220	410-440	6-7
Very hot	230	450	8
Super hot	250-290	475-500	9-10

Cake Dish Sizes

METRIC	IMPERIAL
15cm	6in
18cm	7in
20cm	8in
23cm	9in

Loaf Dish Sizes

METRIC	IMPERIAL
23 x 12cm	09 x 5in
25 x 08cm	10 x 3in
28 x 18cm	11 x 7in

Liquid Measures

METRIC	IMPERIAL	CUP AND SPOON
ml	fl oz	
millilitres	fluid ounce	
5mL	$^1/_6$ fl oz	1 teaspoon
20mL	$^2/_3$ fl oz	1 tablespoon
30mL	1 fl oz	1 tablespoon plus 2 teaspoons
55mL	2 fl oz	$^1/_4$ cup
85mL	3 fl oz	$^1/_3$ cup
100mL	$3^1/_2$ fl oz	$^3/_8$ cup
125mL	$4^1/_2$ fl oz	$^1/_2$ cup
145mL	5 fl oz	$^1/_4$ pint, 1 gill
250mL	$8^3/_4$ fl oz	1 cup
300mL	$10^1/_2$ fl oz	$^1/_2$ pint
350mL	$12^1/_4$ fl oz	$1^1/_2$ cups
400mL	14 fl oz	
500mL	$17^1/_2$ fl oz	2 cups
570mL	20 fl oz	1 pint
1 litre	35 fl oz	$1^3/_4$ pints, 4 cups

Cup Measurements

One cup is equal to the following weights.

	METRIC	IMPERIAL
Almonds, flaked	85g	3oz
Almonds, slivered, ground	125g	$4^1/_2$oz
Almonds, kernels	145g	5oz
Apples, dried, chopped	125g	$4^1/_2$oz
Apricots, dried, chopped	200g	7oz
Breadcrumbs, packet	125g	$4^1/_2$oz
Breadcumbs, soft	55g	2oz
Cheese, grated	125g	$4^1/_2$oz
Choc Bits	155g	$5^1/_2$oz
Coconut, desiccated	85g	3oz
Cornflakes	30g	1oz
Currants	155g	$5^1/_2$oz
Flour	125g	$4^1/_2$oz

	METRIC	IMPERIAL
Fruit, dried (mixed, sultanas etc)	185g	$6^1/_2$oz
Ginger, crystallised, glace	255g	9oz
Honey, treacle, golden syrup	315g	11oz
Mixed Peel	220g	$7^3/_4$oz
Nuts, chopped	125g	$4^1/_2$oz
Prunes, chopped	220g	$7^3/_4$oz
Rice, cooked	155g	5oz
Rice, uncooked	220g	8oz
Rolled Oats	90g	3oz
Sesame Seeds	125g	$4^1/_2$oz
Shortening (butter, margarine)	255g	9oz
Sugar, brown	155g	5oz
Sugar, granulated or caster	255g	9oz
Sugar, sifted icing	155g	5oz
Wheatgerm	55g	2oz

Length

Some of us are still having trouble converting imperial to metric. In this scale measures have been rounded off to the easiest-to-use and most acceptable figures.

To obtain the exact metric equivalent to convert inches to centimetres, multiply inches by 2.54

Therefore 1 inch equals 25.4 millimetres and 1 millimetre equals 0.03937 inches

METRIC	IMPERIAL
mm = millimetres	in = inches
cm = centimetres	ft = feet
5mm, .5cm	1/4in
10mm, 1.0cm	1/2in
20mm, 2.0cm	3/4in
2.5cm	1in
5cm	2in
8cm	3in
10cm	4in
12cm	5in
15cm	6in
18cm	7in
20cm	8in
23cm	9in
25cm	10in
28cm	11in
30cm	1 ft, 12in

Index

96